YOUTH SPORT
AND ACTIVE LEISURE:
THEORY, POLICY
AND PARTICIPATION

Editors:

Anne Flintoff, Jonathan Long
and Kevin Hylton

LSA

108

LSA Publication No. 87

Youth Sport and Active Leisure: Theory, Policy and Participation

First published in 2005 by
Leisure Studies Association
The Chelsea School
University of Brighton
Eastbourne BN20 7SP (UK)

A catalogue record for this book
is available from the British Library.

ISBN: 0 906337 98 4

Layout, cover and typesetting by Myrene L. McFee

Cover photograph:
Grateful thanks are expressed to Marcus Österberg
for permission to adapt his original photograph.

Printed in the UK by
Antony Rowe Ltd, Eastbourne

Contents

EDITORS' INTRODUCTION

YOUTH SPORT AND ACTIVE LEISURE: THEORY, POLICY AND PRACTICE

During the Leisure Studies Association conference on Young People and Active Leisure (July 2004) the minister for Sport Richard Caborn gave an impassioned contribution on sport's ability to deliver the government's agenda. His vision is of a sport strategy that represents a hybrid of what he understands as the best on offer elsewhere: Finland (health), Australia (excellence), France (inclusion). Whether or not those represent quite what he perceives, the goal is a laudable one. Other presenters at the conference both supported and challenged his optimism. As usual the Association provided a critical edge.

Part of the policy agenda relates to the belief that people's mental and physical wellbeing are intimately related to social and lifestyle factors. The government has set itself and others the challenge to widen participation so that 'culture' should be 'for the many, not the few'. What processes might secure this and act to promote social trust and cohesion and mediate conflict? How are expectations and aspirations shaped to encourage the realisation of potential?

Several conference presentations were concerned with policymakers' capacity to understand and relate to young people. Many prevailing understandings are tied into functionalist definitions, hence the enthusiasm for initiatives like the school sport co-ordinators, specialist sports colleges, etc., which are intended to promote sport as a tool for social welfare. Hence the call for initiatives to involve young people in determining policy instead of purely being beneficiaries of provision (or protesting at its lack).

Perhaps it is unfair to suggest that policymakers only to turn to leisure when they are in search of interventions to plug the gaps in other policies; but rather than being valued for itself, sport seems to be valued more for what it can deliver against other social agendas. As part of that instrumental approach there is something akin to the search for the Holy Grail in terms of identifying the best way of establishing school / community links that will secure continued participation in socially acceptable activity. This is evidenced particularly at the moment in terms of sports development. But particularly given the decline in sports participation we have to ask why current efforts are not working?

The theme of the conference was chosen to cover all dimensions of leisure in which young people actively engage, not just the physical. Nonetheless, the majority of presenters did still have sport as their focus though some, like the offerings here from Flintoff and Kirk, did express concern at the hegemony of sport. At the same time as our deliberations, Clint Witchalls noted in the *Guardian* (July 14, 2004) that "sport took away [his] confidence, pride, respect and happiness", and wrote about his desire to "scrap the whole ugly enterprise" of sports day:

> And don't tell me that missing out on that one endless day is going to turn our children into a bunch of lardarses. You don't have to play sport to be healthy. Children ride bikes, climb trees and run around pretending to be Spiderman. They learn dance moves from MTV and dig big holes in the garden to see if they can reach the centre of the earth. All these things keep them fit. They don't need teams, rules, smelly locker rooms and adults blowing whistles at them.

For those of us more favourably disposed to formal forms of active leisure, this is a salutary reminder of the nature of young people's engagement with leisure. Clearly there is a need to critique the hegemony of what is on offer. Diversity and difference in contemporary society have to be acknowledged if practice is to be improved (several presenters, for example, raised issues around the gender relevance of provision). Problems being faced in regard to schools as a site of physical activity development are also reflected in other areas of leisure. The foundations of much of the policy debate are flawed, assuming that everybody subscribes to particular definitions of sport, physical education (PE), the arts, tourism or outdoor activity. As many of the papers identified, there are more alternatives to be considered.

The current interest in social inclusion is founded in a belief that active leisure creates opportunities for personal development — a position which carries more than a hint of the moral arguments previously associated with muscular Christianity. That proviso notwithstanding, that interest does draw attention to the importance of the processes rather than just the products of these leisure activities. But our collection of papers suggests that established conceptions tend to offer opportunities to those already included rather than the excluded. They lend support to Bourdieu's (1993: p. 123) observation that "the probability of practising a sport beyond adolescence declines markedly as one moves down the social hierarchy". Policymakers need to be critical of their own actions and, in trying alternatives, be prepared to risk adverse reactions from the electorate in pursuit of declared goals of inclusion.

This is one of three volumes of papers, presented originally at the Young People and Active Leisure conference of the Leisure Studies Association, held at Leeds Metropolitan University in July 2004. The conference identified several major themes, including Policy and Provision, Engagement and Participation, Alienation and Subculture, Health, Risk and Environment and, finally, Consumption. The papers in this volume are concerned with theory, policy and participation issues surrounding young people's active leisure. There are two parallel publications arising from the conference: one has focused on methodological issues and the evaluation of initiatives designed to engage young people in active leisure (Hylton, Long & Flintoff, 2005). The other reviews youth cultures, legislation and risk taking behaviour, the social construction of sexualised youth identities, and health issues and recreation for youth (Bramham and Caudwell, 2005).

Our reading of the papers included here suggests a series of decentrings: decentring sport within PE, decentring didactic instruction within education, decentring schools within education, decentring positivism in assessing success. This might help to secure a more sympathetic policy discourse.

Section 1: Theorising youth sport and active leisure practice

The first paper by **David Kirk** explores the relationship between the nature and form of school PE, and our broader understandings of physical culture. Kirk provides evidence to show how a sport-based PE, which has dominated the subject since the 1950s, has consistently failed to achieve its primary goal of lifelong participation in physical activity. He is pessimistic that the current reforms in school PE under the overall PE and School Sport Clubs Links Strategy (PESCCL) will help young people develop active lifestyles, since they are informed by traditional and outmoded understandings of physical culture rather than contemporary research about embodiment and empowerment. Kirk argues that three key issues must be addressed if this is to become a reality: change agents in PE must draw on analyses of contemporary forms of physical culture to inform their practice; critical pedagogies must be employed more readily; and finally, programmes need to be gender-relevant.

The paper that follows by **Anne Flintoff** also addresses the social construction of sport-based PE. However, her analysis specifically focuses on the implications of this for girls' and young women's involvement in physical activity. Through tracing the historical development of girls' PE, she shows the shift over time from a practice rooted in education to one which celebrates and centralises performance-orientated, competitive sport. Qualitative research data of the perceptions and attitudes of young women towards PE is presented to show the gap between the realities of many young women's lives and the opportunities on offer from teachers engaged in the delivery of new PE and sport policies. She calls for a return to an educational discourse in PE and for a reinsertion of a critical, gendered analysis if the gendered dimension of the current 'crisis' of young people's inactivity levels is to be adequately addressed.

Joanne Kay continues the theme of challenging dominant constructions of PE and sport provision. This time, the focus is on state funded sport in Canada. The paper presents a framework for exploring the potential of public investment in extreme sport to enhance youth sport participation, and evaluates the usefulness of a social capital approach to policy analysis.

Phil Binks and Bob Snape were also interested in the role of sport for young people within community policies. Far from a joined-up approach, they found a lack of coherence among a confusing patchwork of provision that is a response to shifts in short- and medium-term funding. Competition for this type of project funding frustrates the possibility of coherent long-term development to secure strategic objectives. At the same time, Binks and Snape found that those (such as sports development officers) responsible for delivery had little understanding of the social and political objectives of these programmes.

Section 2: Difference, Young People and Participation

James Lowrey and Tess Kay evaluate the concept of using sport as a vehicle for promoting social inclusion, and Bangladeshi youngsters' responses to a programme of provision explicitly constructed to meet their needs. They found that the Widening Access through Sport (WATS) programme provided a valuable, structured experience of sport education and increased the young people's understanding of the role of the university. However, the authors conclude that the success of such programmes should not be measured solely in terms of progress towards measurable policy goals (i.e. progression to higher education). The positive experiences of the programme, and the contribution it has made to the young people's personal development -- particularly evident with the young Muslim women — should not be lost as a key outcome of the project.

Tess Kay then argues that an understanding of the varying nature and position of the family is essential to understanding young people's participation in sport. Although the nature of South Asian families is changing in Britain, not least because of the increasing educational qualifications of young women, Kay argues that it is the family that remains central to the construction of young Muslim women's identities here. Their involvement in the WATS project, described in the earlier paper by Lowry and Kay (this volume), was wholly conditional on the assurance of their parents that the activities and facilities met the requirements of Islam, and it was the contradictions between these familial constraints and the young women's behaviour on the project — confident and outgoing — that the paper explores. Kay concludes that, rather than "casting off their restrictive traditions", the girls' ethnicity was a source of very positive identity, with their faith a constant reference point for what they were 'allowed' to be. In this way, the young women are actively engaged in identity work in which they are creating a fusion of traditions of their origins, with elements of the majority culture. It is through researching sports experience, Kay argues, that this broader social experience has been revealed.

Phillipa Hunter Jones' paper explores the perceived effects of holiday taking on the health and wellbeing of young people being treated for cancer. Using diaries and interviews to gather the perceptions of young people and professional carers, the paper shows the significance of holiday taking in the process of adolescent development. Taking part with others who had shared the experience of illness was an important part of the success of the holiday, providing a space where they could escape their 'ill person' identity (at least for a while) and develop other aspects of themselves and their identities. The holiday acted as a catalyst for them to regain some independence and self-esteem, as well as make new friends — all-important aspects of the transitions young people make during adolescence. Hunter Jones concludes her paper by calling for more recognition of the importance of holidays in young people's lives with impaired health.

The final paper in this collection, by **Margot Edwards and Kaye Massey**, also focuses on holidays, this time with a focus on family experiences of nature holidays. Drawing on qualitative data collected from mothers and their children, Edwards and Massey explore three key aspects of nature holidays: factors influencing the choice of a nature experience for a family holiday; the impact of mothers' previous nature holidays in determining the objectives of the holiday, and post holiday reflections. The paper concludes with the presentation of a model to explain the decision-making processes for family nature experiences.

References

Bourdieu, P. (1993; first published in French, 1984) *Sociology in question*. London, Sage.

Bramham, P. & Caudwell, J. (2005) *Sport, active leisure and youth cultures* (LSA Publication No. 86). Eastbourne, Leisure Studies Association.

Hylton, K., Long, J. & Flintoff, A. (2005) *Evaluating sport and active leisure for young people* (LSA Publication No. 88). Eastbourne: Leisure Studies Association.

Anne Flintoff, Jonathan Long and Kevin Hylton
Leeds Metropolitan University
February 2005

About the Contributors

Phil Binks is currently a Senior Lecturer in the Sport Leisure and Tourism Management Department at The University of Bolton. He is Programme Leader for the Sports Development degree and involved in the delivery of the MA in Community Sports Development. Recent publications include: P. Binks and D. Morgan (2002) *Sport Equity within the North West. Report for Sport England*; P. Binks (2004) *The Role of Sport Interventions in Community Safety in the North West. Structures, Practice and Issues. Report for Sport England*. Phil is currently engaged in: analysis of Bolton's Positive Activities for Young People (Key Worker) Programme (Report for Connexions); and an assessment of the 'Reczones' Initiative Bolton 2004 (Report for Bolton Met).

Margot Edwards is a Senior Lecturer in the Department of Management and International Business at Massey University, Albany, New Zealand. She has an MSc (Hons) in Zoology from the University of Auckland and has completed a PhD examining the impact of gender on the roles and qualities of elite women's hockey coaches. Her research interests include sport and leisure management, coaching, and leadership. She has recently joined the 'Talent Flow' team at Massey University, which is an international project exploring global migration from a New Zealand context.

Anne Flintoff is Reader in Physical Education and Education Development in the Carnegie Faculty of Sport and Education at Leeds Metropolitan University. She is part of the Gender, Race and Equity Research Group and teaches on undergraduate and post graduate pathways in the sociology of PE and sport. Her major research interests include gender and physical education; contemporary youth sport policy; young people and active lifestyles; PE teacher education; gender and education; feminist theory and sport. She has published widely in PE and sport studies, and is a member of the Editorial Board of Physical Education and Sport Pedagogy.

Kevin Hylton is a Senior Lecturer in the Carnegie Faculty of Sport and Education at Leeds Metropolitan University. He teaches sociology and community studies on the Sport and Recreation Development BA (Hons) and is the course leader for the MA in Sport, Leisure and Equity. Kevin conducts research and consultancies for the Carnegie Research Institute especially in the areas of 'race' and racism in sport. Kevin is co-editor of Sports Development: Policy, Process and Practice, London, Routledge.

Philippa Hunter-Jones is a Senior Lecturer in Tourism Management at Manchester Metropolitan University (School of Food, Consumer, Tourism and Hospitality Management, Old Hall Lane, Manchester, M14 6HR, UK. Email p.a.hunter-jones@mmu.ac.uk). She completed her doctoral study investigating the relationship between holiday-taking and health. Her particular research focus was to qualitatively determine the perceived effects of holiday-taking upon the health and wellbeing of patients treated for cancer. Currently she is involved in a project exploring the relationship between holiday-taking and respite care. Here both the care-recipient and care-giving perspective are under investigation.

Joanne Kay holds a Ph.D. in Sport Sociology from the Université de Montréal. She has taught Sport Sociology at Université de Montreal and Queen's University. She is currently a Senior Policy Analyst and the sport policy research coordinator with Canada's federal government. Kay has extensive experience and an international publication profile in action sport research, having mostly focused on the emergence of these sports in relation to gender, media and corporate culture. Kay's work as a freelance journalist has been featured in local and national media. As an athlete, Kay was a member of Canada's national triathlon team.

Tess Kay is Senior Research Fellow in the Institute of Youth Sport, Loughborough University. She has researched widely in the area of sport and leisure behaviour with particular interests in gender, inclusion and the use of sport in social policy. She is the author with Michael Collins of *Sport and Social Inclusion* (Routledge, 2003). She has a particular interest in the family as a context for leisure and is currently undertaking research into leisure and fatherhood, and into family influences on young people's leisure behaviour in different ethnic groups.

David Kirk joined Leeds Metropolitan University in March 2005 as Dean of the Carnegie Faculty of Sport and Education. He previously held a Chair in Physical Education and Youth Sport at Loughborough University between 1998 and 2005 and was Professor of Human Movement Studies at the University of Queensland, Australia between 1994-1998. Professor Kirk has degrees from the Scottish School of Physical Education, the University of Glasgow and Loughborough University. He was European Editor of the Journal of Curriculum Studies from 1999-2004, and is currently Editor of *Physical Education and Sport Pedagogy*. He received the IOC President's Prize in 2001 for his contribution to research in physical and sport education, and the Outstanding Scholar Award in 2003 from the Research on Instruction and Learning in Physical Education Special Interest Group of the American Educational Research Association.

Jonathan Long was previously Research Director at the Centre for Leisure Research and the Tourism and Recreation Research Unit. Now a professor in the Carnegie Research Institute, he continues to conduct projects for external clients. Recent research has included various works on social inclusion and the benefits of sport and the arts and a suite of projects on racism in sport. He is currently working on the national evaluation of the Local Exercise Action Pilots. Jonathan has been a member of LSA since 1976; a former member of the Executive, Newsletter Editor and conference organiser. He was also on the editorial board of the Journal of the Leisure Association *Leisure Studies* for 15 years, at various times acting as editor and book reviews editor.

James Lowrey is a Senior Research Assistant at the Centre for Public Policy, Northumbria University. His research has focused on black and minority ethnic communities and their experiences of sport and education. He has examined the usefulness of sport as a vehicle for encouraging young people to participate within further and higher education. He is currently working on a national research project focusing on disabled people, supported employment, and social inclusion.

Bob Snape is Principal Lecturer in the Department of Sport, Leisure and Tourism Management at the University of Bolton. His research interests include the political, cultural and social contexts of community sport development and cultural aspects of leisure in the period 1850–1914, particularly those relating to public libraries, museums and art galleries. He has undertaken a number of recent evaluation projects in community development through sport including work on the role of sport in the Community Cohesion Pathfinders and on the promotion of sport participation amongst Asian women in Bolton. He is the current Secretary of the Leisure Studies Association.

Kaye Thorn is a Lecturer within the Department of Management and International Business at Massey University, Albany, New Zealand. She has an MSc in Resource Management, and has spent much of her working career in the fields of environmental management and tourism. Her research interests have integrated these two areas. She is currently enrolled in doctoral studies, examining the implications of the "Brain Drain" on highly skilled New Zealanders.

I

THEORISING YOUTH SPORT
AND ACTIVE LEISURE PRACTICE

PHYSICAL CULTURE, LIFELONG PARTICIPATION AND EMPOWERMENT: TOWARDS AN EDUCATIONAL RATIONALE FOR PHYSICAL EDUCATION

David Kirk

Dean, Carnegie Faculty of Sport and Education
Leeds Metropolitan University

I have read the report and while it is interesting, I must point out that the English idea of sport is such that the English do not like professional professorial discourses on sport. At the same time, I can see that there is some rather interesting information, perhaps, for some countries which are backward in educational matters. [Mr Lloyd, Minister of Education, on the UNESCO report 'The Place of Sport in Education', 1956]

Introduction

During the past five years, physical education and school sport increasingly have been the targets of a raft of government-sponsored initiatives. Indeed, there have been so many new programs and projects that an overarching coordination strategy has been devised in the form of the Physical Education and School Sport and Club Links Strategy (PESSCLS) involving partnerships between eight separate initiatives and associated organisations (Department for Education and Skills, DfES, 2002). To sharpen the point, over £1 billion of public money has been pledged to developments in physical education and school sport during the second term of office of the Blair government. With reform on this scale and at this cost, it would be reasonable to assume that the program has been underpinned by a careful review of the published research in this field. Unfortunately, for the most part, it has not. Although many programs have evaluation components, few if any have been explicitly

3

and intentionally shaped by what we have learned from research, and the overall coordinating strategy is entirely devoid of a research base. It would appear that the attitude of Government to research in physical education may have changed little since Mr Lloyd's statement made in 1956. My fear is that we will experience much innovation but little change.

In this paper, I want to consider the kinds of issues, informed by research, we need to take account of if we are to bring about genuine, authentic change in school physical education that provides educationally worthwhile experiences and outcomes for all young people. My argument is that the current reforms in school physical education are legitimated by imperatives for order, relation and identity contained within the physical cultural discourses of sport, exercise/health and leisure. Since there is no research base to these reforms, however, individuals and organisations central to reform initiatives are less likely to be informed about new ideas and practices beyond their local situations. Moreover, I aim to show in this paper there is an intimate relationship between the public discourses of physical culture and forms of school physical education. In the absence of a systematic program of research, reform agents are less likely to have access to contemporary analyses of public discourse and so the forms of physical education they are able to imagine are more likely to relate to and be legitimated by older and in some cases obsolete dimensions of physical culture (Kirk, 1998a). My proposal is that analyses of contemporary physical culture require the development of forms of physical education based on an educational rationale and aimed at empowerment. I will suggest later in this paper that a primary consideration of physical education for empowerment is that it is built on a critique of contemporary forms of physical culture, that it takes embodiment as its central focus, and that it is gender-relevant. Empowerment involves educating both boys and girls, in the words of Iris Marion Young, "to use their full bodily capacities in free and open engagement with the world", in which the body uses "its real capacity, both as the potentiality of its physical size and strength and as the real skills and coordination which are available to it" (Young, 1980: p. 146).

I begin by arguing that the dominant practice of school physical education at Key Stages 2, 3 and 4 (i.e. in the age range 8–16) is sport-based[1] and that since the mid 1950s it has consistently failed to achieve its primary goal, which is lifelong participation in physical activity. In order to begin to understand why this is so, in the next section I argue that we need to analyse the relationships between the social construction of school knowledge and broader, non-pedagogic forms of public discourse. Following this analysis of the structuring discourses of sport-based physical education I seek to show

how the institutional imperatives of the school itself and its culture of acquisition conspire to sustain sport-based physical education as abstracted and decontextualised knowledge. Finally, on the basis of this critique, I argue for forms of physical education that are situated in young people's lives and within contemporary physical culture.

Sport-based physical education and lifelong participation

There has been a commonplace and widespread belief in the UK and elsewhere since at least the 1930s that one of the main purposes of school physical education is to prepare young people for lifelong physical activity. Since the emergence of sport-based physical education in the 1950s in this country, this belief about the purposes of school physical education has taken a particular form. It has been argued that young people should be introduced to a wide range of physical activities so that they might find at least one in which they might wish to continue to participate throughout their adulthood (Green, 2004). I want to suggest that this argument can bear very little critical scrutiny before it is exposed as being simplistic and naïve, at least in relation to the current forms of sport-based physical education. I will also argue, however, that the goal of lifelong participation is of major consequence within an educational rationale for physical education and empowerment.

First of all, I want to demonstrate the ubiquity of this aim. In the UK, for example, the NCPE claims to develop:

> Learning which leads to increasing competence and, thereby, personal confidence and self-esteem. This provides the basis for lifelong learning in and enjoyment of physical activity and the ability to continue learning independently. (QCA, 1999: p. 1)

Sport England were arguing in 2002 in similar fashion that the Active Schools program:

> Demonstrates Sport England's commitment to encouraging every child to stay physically active for life. It highlights the importance of physical activity as an essential part of a healthy, active lifestyle. (Sport England, 2002: p. 2)

This aim for lifelong participation is not new, nor is it confined to the UK. Foreshadowing the emergence of sport-based physical education, Sir George Newman wrote in the prefatory memorandum to the Board of Education's

1933 Syllabus (known around the world as the Green Book):

> Physical training at school should form the ground work of healthy
> exercise and recreation in after life [sic, life after school]. (Board of
> Education, 1933: p. 8)

In the Australian State of Victoria in 1946, the replacement for the Green Book
— known to teachers as the Grey Book — set out sport-based physical
education in a contemporaneously recognisable form for the first time, and
it was underpinned by the view that:

> The aims of this system of physical education are that each individual
> shall be enabled to develop to his maximum potential and that each
> one shall acquire a sufficient degree of proficiency in at least one form
> of physical activity to enable him to maintain an interest in healthy
> activities throughout his adult life. (Education Department of Victoria,
> 1946: p. vii)

By the early 1970s sport-based physical education and the aspiration of
lifelong learning was well established. In the 1972 Scottish *Curriculum Paper
12*, it was claimed that:

> Through satisfying participation pupils develop positive attitudes
> towards physical activity and are therefore favourably disposed
> towards continuing to participate in appropriate activities in
> later school years and in adult life. (Scottish Education Department,
> 1972: p. 9)

So the aim of life-long participation is commonplace in England, Scotland and
Australia (as just three examples), and has been since at least the 1930s. Given
the durability of this aim, can we conclude that it is in some sense valid? I
want to suggest that the aim of lifelong participation is a valid and proper
aspiration of physical education. Whatever else we might want to claim for
physical education, it seems reasonable to suggest that there will be some
transfer of learning from young people's school experience to their lives
outside the school, and then beyond the school into adulthood. If not, how can
physical educators hope to persuade the general public, politicians and other
interested parties that physical education can deliver the range of individual
and social goods it so often promises, such as skill development, teamwork,
health, and self-esteem. Moreover, surely the most conclusive evidence of
transfer of learning is that people *do* continue to be active beyond their school
careers. Because without *this* outcome, continuing participation, how can we

ever be sure that the various cognitive, physical, affective and social goods adults may display in various life situations, such as team work and so on, are a result of their school physical education experience, and do not derive from some other source or experience? At the same time, as Evans (2004) has cautioned, any educational or other benefits to pupils' lives beyond the school originates in the quality of their physical education experience in school.

Even though I believe the aim of lifelong participation is valid and highly appropriate, the available evidence, ironically, does not support it. However we look at the issue, there is very little evidence to suggest that, since the first appearance of sport-based physical education in universal secondary schooling in the early 1950s, programs have been able to achieve their aim of promoting lifelong participation. In the UK, the DCMS report 'A sporting future for all' highlighted once again the importance of life-long participation and commented that "People lose interest as they get older, reducing participation and diminishing the pool of talent" (DCMS, 2001: p. 5). Sport England reproduced on their web page the following table (see Table 1) from two separate studies in the mid 1990s that show a clear disparity between the activities children are likely to experience at school, and the activities adults are likely to participate in.

Table 1   *Top sports participation facts*

* Adults Participating at Least Once a Month, 1996:			** School Children Participating at Least Once a Year, 1994:		
1.	Walking	44.5%	1.	Swimming	85%
2.	Swimming	14.6%	2.	Cycling	79%
3.	Keep fit/Yoga	12.3%	3.	Athletics (Track&Field)	81%
4.	Snooker/ Billiards	11.3%	4.	Gymnastics (Gym)	69%
5.	Cycling	11%	5.	Football	77%
6.	Weight training	5.6%	6.	Rounders	75%
7.	Football	4.8%	7.	Tennis	67%
8.	Golf	4.7%	8.	Walking (>1hr.)/Hiking	62%
9.	Running	4.5%	9.	Cricket	59%
10.	Tenpin bowls/ skittles	3.4%	10.	Cross Country/ Jogging	51%

Source: Office of Population Censuses and Surveys, Living in Britain 1996)
Source: Sports Council, Young People and Sport in England, 1994)

The patterns evident in this simple table can be found in other surveys of adult participation. For example, in Australia, surveys of participation in physical activity conducted between 1984 and 1994 show that, of people aged 14 to 24, walking, swimming, aerobics, jogging and cycling rank substantially higher than all other activities (ABS, 1994; ASC, 1991; DASET, 1992; DASETT, 1988). As people in contemporary Australia get older, walking becomes more popular, as does fishing, golf and lawn bowls, with tennis and boating holding their own across age groups, while team games and other sports pale into insignificance. These surveys tell the same story consistently and persuasively — only a tiny minority of Australians and Britons who lead an active lifestyle in adulthood play team games or any other competitive sport. Yet team games and sports, or an impoverished version of them, take the lion's share of time in school physical education programs (Almond, 1997; Penney & Evans, 1999).

And contrary to recent media reports, low levels of participation in traditional games and sports is not a recent problem. We have little solid information on sports participation among adults prior to the late 1980s. But there is some evidence to suggest that levels of participation were low — much to the frustration of the writers of the Wolfenden Report of 1958 for example (in Kirk, 1992a) — even after the introduction of sport-based physical education to the masses through universal secondary education in the late 1940s/ early 1950s. For instance, a CCPR (1961) survey in 1960 of working class school leavers' interest in continuing to play sport they had experienced at school reported that, although many young people said they intended to continue to participate, only 20% had actually made arrangements to do so two weeks before leaving. Roberts (1996) cites a study from 1971 that shows a third of boys and over half the girls in a 2683 strong sample of school-leavers from south-east Lancashire did no out-of school sport at all. Meanwhile, in Australia, Brian Nettleton published a paper in 1968 based on a secondary analysis of surveys of the leisure pursuits of Australians, including their involvement in sport and exercise. The studies he cited date from 1945 through to 1966 and included rural and provincial settings as well as cities. Nettleton admits that these surveys were not necessarily well designed, but he claims that 'they present a weight of qualitative evidence which suggests a society in which the proportion of individuals who participate in active sport during their leisure hours is small, and that this proportion diminishes with age' (Nettleton, 1968). The weight of evidence, covering a period from 1945 to 1966, convinced Nettleton that 'homo-sedens Australis' was the rule rather than the exception.

So even though there appears to be face validity to the notion of lifelong participation as a goal of school physical education, there is little evidence to suggest the goal has been realised. I will return to the concept of transfer of learning later in this paper, since it is quite central to the proposal that the lifelong participation goal has face validity. In the meantime, we might ask why has physical education failed so apparently consistently and spectacularly since the 1950s to achieve this ubiquitous goal? Part of the answer lies in the nature of sport-based physical education, an issue I will come to shortly. Part of the answer also lies in the forms of public discourse that legitimate particular forms of the subject in schools.

Public discourse and the social construction of school subjects

The concept of the social construction of physical education is central to this part of my argument, and needs to be defined. The concept draws in part on the field of curriculum history, developed and elaborated through the work of Ivor Goodson (1988) and others. Goodson argued that the rise and fall of school subjects is not a process of natural evolution but is instead the outcome of conflict and contestation between vying interest groups. Goodson uses examples from subjects such as Geography and Modern Studies to make his point, and there now exist curriculum histories of most other school subjects that provide strong empirical support for his hypotheses. My own work in this area in the UK and Australia (Kirk, 1992a; Kirk, 1998b) shows that physical education is no exception; indeed, in many respects it is an exemplary case for the application of Goodson's theories. The social construction of physical education refers, then, to the organisation of school knowledge according to the preferences, interests and cultures of vying individuals and groups of people.

In a paper closely related to the project of curriculum history, Anne Williams (1985) explained how we might understand constraints on innovation in physical education. Drawing on the work of curriculum theorist Bill Reid, she argued that for any successful innovation to take place, there has to be a close match between the 'organisational categories' that define the form and content of school physical education within educational institutions and the 'institutional categories' of sport and leisure external to education systems that legitimate school physical education. She argued that a health-related fitness form of physical education had rapidly consolidated a place in British schools in the early 1980s in large part because this organisational form of the subject matched various legitimating publics' interests in and the understanding of physical education in terms of its relationship to health and fitness.

Basil Bernstein's (1990) work on the social construction of pedagogic discourse provides the conceptual tools to investigate with greater precision the relationship, flagged up by the curriculum history project and curriculum analyses such as Williams's, between school (pedagogic) knowledge and public (non-pedagogic) knowledge. Two key concepts in Bernstein's theory are instructional discourse and regulative discourse. The instructional discourse of school physical education takes specific and substantive forms depending on the settings in which it is instantiated and practiced, and is concerned primarily with making sense of the transmission and acquisition of knowledge in the physical domain. Regulative discourse is made up in part by what I have elsewhere called 'physical culture' (Kirk, 1999a), a range of discursive practices concerned with the maintenance, representation and regulation of the body, in contemporary Britain centred on three highly codified, institutionalised forms of physical activity — sport, leisure and exercise/health.

In contrast to instructional discourse, which is a specific pedagogic form of knowledge, regulative discourse is formed of an array of discursive practices that are not necessarily specific to school subjects, but contain within them imperatives for order, relation and identity within such specific pedagogic forms. According to Bernstein, pedagogic discourse is a means of describing how regulative discourse and instructional discourse relate to each other; Bernstein's favoured descriptor is that instructional discourse is 'embedded' in regulative discourse, suggesting an organic relationship that involves inextricable connection, constant change and mutual though not necessarily even adaptation.

Bernstein proposes that distributive, recontextualising and evaluation rules operate within three fields or spheres of action, the distributive rules in a primary context of the production of discourse, the evaluation rules in a secondary context of the reproduction of discourse, and the recontextualising rules in a third, recontextualising context. As we can see in Diagram 1, in each of these contexts specific agents and agencies operate according to these rules. Bernstein sees the primary context as the place in which the 'yet to be thought or imagined' becomes reality and so where new knowledge is created. Much of this work is done in universities and other knowledge production agencies. The secondary context is centrally concerned with the reproduction of these new ideas once that they are 'thinkable', and this work takes place mainly in

Diagram 1　　*Bernstein's 3 fields of production, reproduction and recontextualisation of pedagogic discourse*

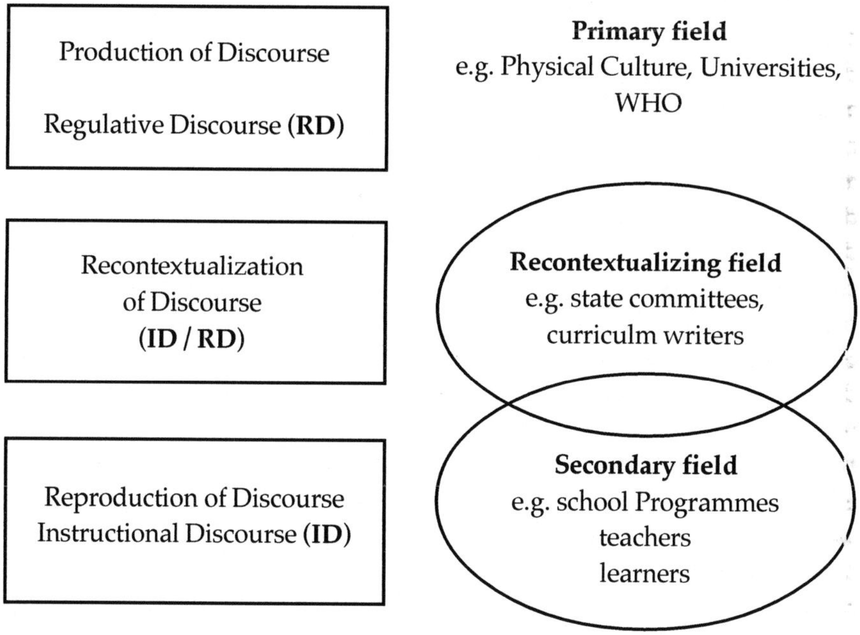

Production of Discourse Regulative Discourse (**RD**)	**Primary field** e.g. Physical Culture, Universities, WHO
Recontextualization of Discourse (**ID / RD**)	**Recontextualizing field** e.g. state committees, curriculm writers
Reproduction of Discourse Instructional Discourse (**ID**)	**Secondary field** e.g. school Programmes teachers learners

educational institutions such as schools. The recontextualising context is concerned primarily with the mediation of discursive resources between the primary and secondary contexts, and much of this work is done by specialised agencies such as state departments of education and allied agencies such as, in the UK, the Qualifications Curriculum Authority, professional associations, educational media, and the Youth Sport Trust.

The construction of forms of school physical education (instructional discourse) out of the juxtapositioning of the discursive practices of sport, exercise/health and leisure that constitute physical culture (regulative discourse) takes place primarily within Bernstein's recontextualising field. This process takes the form of producing national curricula and other syllabi and policies. When new physical education projects and programs are implemented in schools, that is, within Bernstein's secondary context of reproduction, they reproduce those aspects of physical culture that were selected and organised by agents in the recontextualising field. This location by Bernstein of the instructional discourse/ regulative discourse interface within the recontextualising field is therefore of fundamental importance to our understanding of the forms school physical education can take, because it is here that educational change agents make sense of the discursive resources that constitute physical culture and select particular aspects of these resources to make a form of school physical education.

It is within the recontextualizing field, at the interface of instructional discourse/ regulative discourse, that some of the most vigorous struggles have taken place over the form of school physical education. In the 1950s and early 1960s in the UK, a masculinised form of sport-based physical education rose to prominence, displacing both the older Swedish Gymnastics and more recent and feminised educational gymnastics forms of physical education (Fletcher, 1984; Kirk, 1992a). It was during this time that the notion of lifelong participation as a central aspiration of sport-based physical education gained momentum, legitimated by physical cultural discourses such as 'sport for all' and the 'leisure society'. I have argued elsewhere that this form of physical education, as the mainstay of secondary school programs, has remained more or less intact since the 1950s (Kirk, 1992a; Kirk, 1998a). It has managed to accommodate and subsume a health-related exercise form of physical education during the 1980s and 1990s as various waves of concern over obesity have formed what Robert Crawford (1980) calls the new health consciousness public discourse. And, as recent research by Curtner-Smith (1999), Green (1998), Penney & Evans (1999) suggests, it has also managed to survive and thrive in the context of the national curriculum.

The application of Bernstein's theory provides us with one other important insight. While the instructional discourse of sport-based physical education has endured in much the same form for around 50 years, the forms of physical culture that legitimated it at the time of its emergence in the 1950s and 1960s have changed dramatically. Sport as a contemporary discursive form is barely recognisable compared to its 1960s counterpart, in terms of its commercialisation, mediasation and commodification (Maguire & Young, 2002). Concomitantly, notions of sport for all and the leisure society that first sustained the emerging sport-based physical education have been radically reworked. We might ask then, of the change agents working in the recontext-ualizing field and involved in the current raft of initiatives in school physical education, which forms of physical cultural discourses have they selected in the construction of new projects and programs? To what extent have their practices been informed by research on contemporary physical culture and young people's engagements with sport, exercise/ health and leisure discourses? We might also ask what this analysis means for young people's experiences of current forms of school physical education? In order to answer this question, I turn to Lave and Wenger's (1991) situated learning theory and in particular Lave's analysis of the problem of transfer of school learning to life beyond the school gates and on into adulthood.

The school as an institution and the transfer of learning

As I noted earlier, the notion of the possibility of transfer of learning from school to life beyond the school is central to the lifelong participation goal. I suggested that without some form of transfer of the individual and social goods physical education claims to provide, it may be very difficult to justify physical education's existence. This is because, as I've argued, in the absence of continuing participation in physical activity, there is little evidence that these goods are necessarily derived from young people's experiences of physical education. It is significant then that the question of the transfer of learning has featured prominently within the literature on educational learning theory, and has been of particular interest to situated learning researchers.

Much of the research on situated learning or situated cognition in schools has been concerned with mathematics and science. Much criticism of traditional mathematics teaching, for example, has targeted the view that appropriate mathematical learning is abstracted from specific contexts. Lave (1997) referred to this view of learning as the 'culture of acquisition', in which it is assumed that it is the task of the school to transmit to children the valued accumulated factual knowledge of a society, and it is children's task to acquire and reproduce this knowledge. She claimed it is further assumed that:

> Cognitive benefits follow only when the process of learning is removed from the fields in which what is learned is to be applied. This belief underlies standard distinctions between formal and informal learning, so-called context-free and context-embedded learning, or logical and intuitive understanding. Schooling is viewed as the institutional site for decontextualizing knowledge so that, abstracted, it may become general and hence generalizable, and therefore transferable to situations of use in the 'real' world. (Lave, 1997: p. 18)

Drawing on ethnographic studies of shoppers and dieters, Lave suggested that their practices for solving problems of calculation bear little resemblance to the ways in which children are taught mathematics in school. Citing a further study of a school mathematics class, she showed that children could produce correct solutions to problems without using the strategies taught by their teachers. She proposed that the process of doing mathematics in school is in itself a situated practice, and argued that this in turn makes the possibility of transfer of school knowledge to other situations in the real world highly problematic.

There is a striking parallel between this critique of school mathematics and sport-based physical education. Writing in an American context, Siedentop (1994) argues that physical education has been decontextualised and abstracted in a similar way to school mathematics. He says:

> Skills are taught in isolation rather than as part of the natural context of executing strategy in game-like situations. The rituals, values and traditions of a sport that give it meaning are seldom even mentioned, let alone taught in ways that students can experience them. The affiliation with a team or group that provides the context for personal growth and responsibility in sport is noticeably absent in physical education. The ebb and flow of a sport season is seldom captured in a short-term sport instruction unit ... physical education teaches only isolated sport skills and less-than-meaningful games. (Siedentop, 1994: pp. 7–8)

This decontextualisation of learning is made possible by what Ennis (1999) calls, again in an American context, the multi-activity curriculum model of school physical education. This model is characterised by short units of activity (6 to 10 lessons), minimal opportunities for sustained instruction, little accountability for learning, weak or non-existent transfer of learning across lessons, units and year levels, few policies to equalise participation between boys and girls (in co-ed) and high-low skilled players, and a student social system that undermines teacher authority. The practice of sport-based physical education in the UK may not match precisely the situation in the USA described by Siedentop and Ennis. However, as studies in the UK by Green (2002), Curtner-Smith (1999), Penney and Evans (1999) and others show, any differences in practice between the two countries may be a matter of degree rather than of kind.

In similar fashion to the critique of school mathematics, there is a large body of evidence to suggest that this decontextualised approach to physical education disadvantages girls (Flintoff & Scraton, 2001; Williams & Bedward, 2001), particular ethnic groups (Vescio *et al.*, 1999; Benn, 1996), and alienates motorically less gifted (Carlson, 1995) and disabled young people (Kosma *et al.*, 2002), while reproducing and celebrating hegemonic masculinity (Nilges, 1998; Wright, 1997). Moreover, addressing the issue of transfer of learning directly, we have already noted that a ubiquitous goal of sport-based physical education is to promote lifelong participation in physical activity. The mult-activity, sport-based curriculum model is the consequence of this aspiration since it is based on the assumption that, presented with a taste of a wide range of activities, young people will find one or two that will sustain their participation.

Given these parallels between critiques of other forms of school knowledge such as maths, and physical education, we might ask to what extent transfer of learning is possible? In the case of physical education, I suggest we are forced to conclude that there appears to be very limited potential for transfer if we accept as evidence the very small numbers of adults who continue to participate in the sports and games they experienced at school. Even when we broaden the term sport to physical activity, as proposed by Deem & Gilroy (1998), we find that many adults who enjoy a physically active life do so despite negative experiences at school, or else participate in activities in adulthood that were never available to them at school (Flintoff and Scraton, 2001). And, if further evidence is needed, we can recall the sizable literature that suggests some, perhaps many, children are dissatisfied and some alienated by their immediate experiences of physical education. There is evidence to suggest that even among the young people who claim to enjoy their sport-based physical education experience, not all of them — to use Lave's (1997: p. 18) term in relation to the culture of acquisition — can be said to 'get it' (Kirk *et al.*, 2000), to make sense of their experiences of school activities.

The fact that school learning is in itself a situated practice, as Lave (1997) suggests, in no small part contributes to this problem of transfer. Since its emergence in the modern era, from at least the 1880s and the consolidation in many western countries of mass compulsory schooling, the school has sought to impose order on the bodies of children by manipulating space (e.g., in the arrangement of the classroom) and time (e.g., in the form of the timetable) (Kirk, 1999b). The school thus has its own institutional imperatives for social order that emerged from a particular set of conditions at a particular time. Although those conditions have changed since the late nineteenth century, and although schools have experimented with ways of manipulating these coordinates of time and space, the imperatives for the production of compliant and productive bodies have altered little in the practice of schooling. As Lave (1997) notes, advocates for the culture of acquisition made a virtue out of these institutional imperatives in relation to the abstraction and organisation of knowledge, suggesting that the abstracted nature of school knowledge was no accidental by-product of the imperative for social order but instead a matter of strategic design.

Towards an educational rationale: physical education for empowerment

I have argued to this point that the dominant form of school physical education since the 1950s has been sport-based physical education. The available evidence on adult participation in physical activities suggests that sport-based physical education has failed to achieve its goal of lifelong participation, even though the goal itself has face validity. Why has sport-based physical education continued to be the dominant form of physical education in schools, despite this failure, and despite challenges from health-related exercise programs since the early 1980s, the development of a national curriculum in the early 1990s and, more recently since the late 1990s, a raft of reform projects and programs? I answered firstly that since there was no research base underpinning the NCPE or the most recent initiatives, change agents in Bernstein's recontextualising field have been working with out of date conceptions of the physical cultural discourses of sport, leisure and exercise/health, the discourses out of which sport-based physical education is constructed and by which it claims cultural legitimacy. Secondly, I answered that the culture of acquisition within the school itself as an institution, with its imperatives for social order, support sport-based physical education as an abstracted form of knowledge. Critiques of the culture of acquisition from a situated learning perspective suggest that the possibilities for transfer of learning of school knowledge to life beyond the school are limited. In order for transfer of learning to take place so that school knowledge and its public discourse correlates are in Williams's (1985) terms closely aligned, requires not merely a reconfiguration of school knowledge, but also a re-configuration of power relations between teachers and learners and between learners themselves.

My view is that the discourses of sport, leisure and exercise/ health will continue to act as the regulative discourse of school physical education (Evans, 2004; Maguire, in press). What is required in order to develop new forms of physical education that realise the possibility of transfer of learning, of lifelong participation and empowerment is a closer alignment between current forms of physical cultural discourse and school physical education, and wider use of new pedagogical strategies that challenge the culture of acquisition in schools. I want to consider three issues that I believe to be central to this task.

The first issue is that change agents in the recontextualizing field need to draw on analyses of contemporary forms of physical culture. There is a wealth of material readily available to curriculum planners and policy makers in the sociology of sport, leisure and health literatures, in sport and leisure policy, and in related fields such as cultural studies and youth studies (see Green, 2004). To take just one example, sociological analyses reveal the extent to which sport as a discursive practice has changed between the 1950s and the present time. Prior to the mass availability of television in the 1960s, sport could only be experienced live, as a participant or spectator, or through the print media or cinema newsreels. Television had a massive impact on forms of engagement with sport, leading to the development of media sports such as one day cricket, to the mass global availability of sport as entertainment, and to the commodification of sport (Maguire, in press; Sage, 2002).

The nature of sport as a commodity is highly significant in the lives of young people. In the process of their engagements with sport, young people do not merely 'participate' physically. They are also consumers of the commercialised and commodified products of sport, most obviously in terms of owning sports wear and equipment, but also in terms of identification with particular sports and particular sports teams and individuals. Since physical culture provides the discursive resources for making sense of activities such as sport, young people construct identities utilising these resources, sometimes in highly idiosyncratic, subversive and productive ways as well as in class and gender specific, conformist and reproductive ways (Renold, 1997; Walker, 1988).

My first point then is that new forms of school physical education cannot ignore such shifts in the meaning of sport as a cultural practice. If Bernstein is right to argue that the instructional discourse of school subjects is embedded in regulative discourses such as (in this case) sport, and if analyses of contemporary sport reveal its commodification, school physical education must be cognisant of sport as a commodity. Indeed, it is only through so doing that physical education can create a possibility for transfer of learning and claim to have cultural relevance and legitimacy. For example, it is important to note that since the late 1970s the body has featured increasingly in the sociology of sport, leisure, and health, and more broadly in cultural studies. There are at least three issues of importance here for physical educators to consider. The first of these, as Featherstone (1982) and others have pointed out, is the emergence of the body as a site for consumption and as a commodity in itself. The second is Shilling's (1993) argument that through the 1980s and 1990s, the body has become an individual project requiring work that takes various forms, such as exercise, nutrition, cosmetics and fashion, and even surgery. The third issue is the part physical training, exercise and sport themselves have played historically in the social regulation and normalisation of the body (Kirk, 1998b). I suggest this increasing prominence of the body in culture has huge significance for physical education given the oppressive potential of processes such as commodification and regulation.

By reconceptualising young people's participation in physical activity as a question of their engagements with physical culture (Wright *et al.*, 2003), it becomes possible to see how the construction of identities is embedded in a range of cultural forces such as commodification and globalisation, localism and tradition. A key task of physical education then becomes empowerment, given the oppressive as well as facilitative dimensions of processes such as commodification and regulation. These matters suggest to me the need for consideration of a second issue for physical education, which is the place of a critical pedagogy.

There has been a growing literature on critical pedagogy in physical education since at least the mid 1980s, the most recent contribution being a collection of edited papers by Wright *et al.* (2004). This literature suggests that the key benefit of a critical pedagogy in physical education for young people is that it seeks to assist them to see beyond the obvious or the surface level of physical culture (Macdonald, 2002). This is important, as I have already noted, since physical culture has become increasingly more complex through processes of professionalisation, mediaisation, commercialism and commodification. A critical pedagogy seeks to empower young people by assisting them to make connections between their own life experiences and broader but less visible social process such as the social construction of gender or the relationships between money, media and power. One of the main methods for conducting critical pedagogy is to assist young people to dis-articulate and re-articulate potentially oppressive communications that do ideological work (e.g. a slender body is a healthy body; a muscular body is masculine, not feminine) (Kirk, 1992b).

At the same time, a critical pedagogy cannot be divorced from actual participation in physical activities, although the specific activities that make up physical education programmes would need to be carefully selected according to the perceived needs of young people and the context of their application. There are some examples available in the literature of how critical pedagogy can be carried out in, about and through physical activity (e.g. Kinchin and O'Sullivan, 2003). Gard's (2004) recent work on dance as movement, art and culture attempts to show how it might be possible to move across the continuum from technical proficiency and personal reflection through to social analysis and ideological critique and do this through physical activity experiences. Gard uses dance as movement education, dance as art and dance as culture to provide examples of how problem solving and critical inquiry can be centred on the experience of embodiment. Work of this kind presents a radical challenge to sport-based physical education.

A third issue that is central to the task of reforming physical education is the development of gender-relevant programs. While factors such as age, ethnicity and dis-ablebodiedness are also of key relevance to the production of empowering physical education programs, the part physical education has played historically in the social construction of hegemonic masculinity and the reproduction of inequitable gender relations (Penney, 2002), suggests that gender must be a key focus. Patricia Vertinsky (1992) has argued that to move toward gender-sensitive physical education, teachers must place issues of gender centre-stage and teach explicitly about the social construction of gender in order to achieve greater gender equity.

Gender-relevant programs do not imply a preference for either co-educational or single-sex classes. Indeed, gender-relevant physical education would embrace either option depending on the specific contexts in which they were to be applied. The key principal, instead, is the explicit acknowledgement that physical education is concerned with reproducing and legitimating particular femininities and masculinities. Since the body is a primary medium for the learning that takes place in physical education classes, subject matter and teaching styles would be selected intentionally to foster learning outcomes that legitimate a wide range of embodied femininities and masculinities. Gender-relevant programs would also seek to provide young people with the skills and knowledge to critique and dis-articulate oppressive, hegemonic gender stereotypes in and through physical activity as a medium.

Some feminist scholars have questioned the need for girls to engage in sport as part of a gender-relevant physical education program. Deem and Gilroy (1998), for example, question the compulsory nature of physical education in schools and point out that physical activity is promoted as a voluntary leisure pursuit outside schools. Others, such as Vertinsky (1992) and Wright (1996) have argued that sport could be replaced by non-competitive activities such as life-time wellness programs and dance. Flintoff & Scraton (2001) propose that there needs to be a broadening of activities beyond traditional competitive sports, greater choice for girls about how they dress and what they do in physical education, and more emphasis on issues that interest girls such as health-related exercise. Williams & Bedward (2001) support these suggestions, and claim that the need is for more flexibility and choice for girls prior to age 14 in order for school practice to be consistent with the Government's inclusive curriculum policy. Some of these proposals for action to reform physical education for girls may imply that sport might best be eliminated from programs altogether.

One alternative form of physical education investigated by Humberstone (1990) did just this, since it took place at an outdoor adventure centre. Boys and girls in small co-educational groups attended the centre with their teachers for one week. The curriculum involved land and water based activities that included considerable physical challenges, a high dependency on team work, and some risk-taking. Humberstone reported that the boys and girls developed a more sensitive understanding of themselves and each other following their outdoor-adventure experiences. These non-sport activities provided the boys in particular with opportunities to re-think their views of girls' physical competence.

While Williams & Bedward (2001) support the kind of alternative curriculum described by Humberstone, they argue against removing sport from physical education programs, citing evidence from their own research that many girls in England would like to play traditional boys-only sports such as football but are not permitted to do so. In support of this view, Lois Bryson (1990) observed that not all physical activities are equally implicated in maintaining the gender order, at least in terms of their exclusivity as a 'male preserve' (Theberge, 1985), even where they involve competition. Bryson cites the various codes of football as sports that symbolize hegemonic masculinity. But she identifies a range of other sports such as badminton, athletics, swimming and golf that do not represent the same masculinist values. Bryson suggests it is possible for girls and boys to participate in sport activities without necessarily practising or being oppressed by hegemonic masculinity.

As interest in masculinity and sport has developed, increasingly researchers have been drawn to concerns that boys and not girls are the under-performing group in schools and the most likely group of young people to be at-risk and marginalised in society (Connell, 1996). While researchers such as Connell show convincingly that men as a group continue to be socially and economically privileged over women, the question 'what about the boys?' has generated important educational issues for schools as well as much emotive reaction. Some policy initiatives have been based on the notion that if sport is 'where the boys are', then this is where community workers should start in their attempts to develop more tolerant and responsible forms of masculinity (Hickey & Fitzclarence, 1999). But for such approaches to be effective, they need to break some of the commonplace and deeply felt associations between sports such as football and the traits of dominant masculinity, including violence and homophobia (Skelton, 2000).

Other research around the issue of masculinity and sport has also begun to raise searching questions about boys' and men's physical and emotional experiences of sport, such as their experiences of both pain and pleasure through physical contact with other males (Gard & Meyenn, 2000; Light, 1998). Such issues are potentially controversial in a school context in particular since they touch on topics that have up until now been taboo. As studies continue to be conducted around the question of boys' experiences of physical education and their contribution to the social construction of masculinity, there is likely to be increasing pressure on physical educators to address issues of pleasure, sexuality, power, and related topics (Beckett, 1998).

Consideration of alternative forms of pedagogy within gender-relevant physical education employing a critical pedagogy provides a perspective on how the culture of acquisition in schools might be challenged. Alternatives to sport-based physical education such as Gard's approach to dance as movement, art and culture, Ennis's Sport for Peace, Kinchin and O'Sullivan's Cultural Studies model, and Oliver and Lalik's integration of physical education and critical literacy provide possibilities for learning that connect the physical and the personal to the social and the cultural dimensions of experience. It is significant to note that each of these alternatives seeks to contextualise and to customise subject matter, teaching styles and learning outcomes to fit specific locales.

Conclusion

I have tried to show in this paper why a particular form of school physical education has remained dominant for the past 50 years, despite its apparent failure to achieve one of its primary goals of lifelong participation. More than this, I argued that the forms of physical culture that construct and legitimate sport-based physical education are already in many respects dated or even obsolete, captured in notions popular in the 1960s and 1970s such as sport for all and the leisure society. My view is that sport-based physical education will continue to dominate school practices until change agents working in Bernstein's recontextualizing field draw on the resources provided by analyses of the contemporary physical cultural practices of sport, leisure and exercise/health which form the regulative discourse in which versions of school physical education are embedded. I concluded by arguing that in addition to bringing the instructional discourse of physical education into closer alignment with contemporary physical culture, the increasing prominence in the public domain of processes of socially constructing the body require the development of a critical pedagogy within gender-relevant forms of physical education aimed at empowerment.

On the basis of this analysis, I have little confidence that the current raft of programs and projects that fall under the rubric of PESSCLS can bring about genuine reform of sport-based physical education. With no program of scholarship informing this process there is little possibility of bringing school physical education out of the mid twentieth century and into the new millennium. As Barrie Houlihan (2000) pointed out, school physical education is a crowded policy space, and the voices that are heard tend to be those that can tap simple and emotive messages that the general public can understand and will readily support. Hence we see the juggernaut of the obesity crisis discourse gaining increasing momentum despite an absence of evidence on almost every key issue, such as the claim that sedentary behaviour is on the increase and that it displaces physical activity, or even the foundational assumption that there is a causal relationship between sedentary behaviour and physical fitness in children (Harris *et al.*, 2004; Marshall *et al.*, 2003). Moreover, as policy for physical education and sport is increasingly drawn into the orbit of government ministers and their departments and specialist advisers (Houlihan & White, 2002), the space for a scholarly program to inform reform greatly diminishes. We need only consider the chapter on physical education in Game Plan (DCMS/ Strategy Unit, 2002) written by the Prime Minister's own policy unit where there is almost a complete omission of references to any physical education research worthy of scholarly note to see the extent of the challenge that faces physical education researchers.

Clearly we need a detailed program of research into the current and recent projects and programs under the umbrella of PESSCLS in order to judge the extent to which they have met their own goals and the needs and interests of young people in schools. We will of course have to wait for some time before we can apply the ultimate test to these innovations in physical education, in terms of the lifelong participation of young people currently in school. However, I would suggest that we cannot and should not have to wait for another fifty years to conclude that the current round of initiatives have failed to deliver this outcome. Careful and ongoing scholarly analyses of physical culture should equip us to judge here and now the cultural relevance and legitimacy of new forms of physical education and their likely potential to realise key educational outcomes such as empowerment.

Note

1   There are various forms of physical education in schools depending on Key Stage and context. The label sport-based physical education is meant to refer to a general characterisation of a set of dominant discursive practices. This is not to say this practice is uncontested by teachers in specific places at specific times — see eg. Kirk (1992a) for a historical perspective on the emergence of sport-based physical education in post World War 2 Britain.

References

Almond, L. (1997) 'Generating a new vision for physical education', pp. 7–20 in Almond, L. (ed) *Physical education in schools*. London: Kogan Page (2nd Edition).

Australian Bureau of Statistics (1994) *Participation in sporting and physical recreational activities, Queensland.* Brisbane: Author.

Australian Sports Commission (1991) *Sport for young Australians: Widening the gateways to participation.* Canberra: Author.

Department of the Arts, Sport, the Environment, Tourism and Territories (1988) *Physical activity levels of Australians.* Canberra: AGPS.

Department of the Arts, Sport, the Environment and Territories (1992) *Summary of the pilot survey of the fitness of Australians* Canberra: AGPS.

Benn, T. (1996) 'Muslim women and physical education in initial teacher training', *Sport, Education and Society* Vol. 1, No. 1: pp. 5–22.

Bernstein, B. (1990) *The structuring of pedagogic discourse: Volume IV, class, codes and control.* London: Routledge.

Board of Education (1933) *Syllabus of physical training for schools*. London: HMSO.

Bryson, L. (1990) 'Challenges to make hegemony in sport', pp. 173–184 in Messner, M.A. & Sabo, D.F. (eds) *Sport, men and the gender order: Critical feminist perspectives.* Champaign: Human Kinetics.

Carlson, T.B. (1995) 'We hate gym: Student alienation from physical education', *Journal of Teaching in Physical Education* 14: pp. 467–477.

Central Council for Physical Recreation (1961) 'A survey in the Eastern counties of England on the sports interests of secondary modern school leavers', *The Leaflet* Vol. 62, No. 3: pp. 23–24.

Crawford, R. (1980) 'Healthism and the medicalization of everyday life', *International Journal of Health Services* 7, pp. 663–680.

Curtner-Smith, M.D. (1999) 'The more things change, the more they stay the same: Factors influencing teachers' interpretations and delivery of the National Curriculum Physical Education', *Sport, Education and Society* Vol. 4, No. 1: pp. 75–98.

Deem, R. & Gilroy, S. (1998) 'Physical activity, life-long learning and empowerment — situating sport in women's leisure', *Sport, Education and Society* Vol. 3, No. 1: pp. 89–104.

DCMS/ Strategy Unit (2002) *Game Plan: A strategy for delivering the Government's sport and physical activity objectives.* http://www.strategy.gov.uk/2002/sport/report.shtmlDepartment of Culture, Media and Sport (2001) *A sporting future for all.* London: Author.

Department for Education and Skills(2002) *Learning through PE and sport.* Annesley: Author.

Education Department of Victoria (1946) *Physical education for Victorian schools.* Melbourne: Author.

Ennis, C.D. (1999) 'Creating a culturally relevant curriculum for disengaged girls', *Sport, Education and Society* 4(1): pp. 31–50.

Evans, J. (2004) 'Making a difference? Education and 'ability' in physical education', *European Physical Education Review* Vol. 10, No. 1: pp. 95–108.

Featherstone, M. (1982) 'The body in consumer culture', *Theory, Culture and Society* 7: pp. 131–162.

Flintoff, A. & Scraton, S. (2001) 'Stepping into active leisure? Young women's perceptions of active lifestyles and their experiences of school physical education', *Sport, Education and Society* Vol. 6, No. 1: pp. 5–21.

Fletcher, S. (1984) *Women first: The female tradition in English Physical Education, 1880-1980.* London: Althone.

Gard, M. (2004) in Wright, J., Macdonald, D. & Burrows, L. (eds) *Critical Inquiry and Problem-Solving in Physical Education.* London: Routledge.

Goodson, I (1988) *The making of curriculum: Collected essays.* Lewes: Falmer.

Green, K. (2004) 'Physical education, lifelong learning and 'the couch potato society'. *Physical Education and Sport Pedagogy* Vol. 9, No. 1: pp. 73–86.

Green, K. (2002).Physical education teachers in their figurations: A sociological analysis of everyday "philosophies"', *Sport, Education and Society* Vol. 7, No. 1: pp. 65–84.

Green, K. (1998) 'Philosophies, ideologies and the practice of physical education', *Sport, Education and Society* Vol. 3, No. 2: pp. 125–143.

Harris, J., Cale, L., Bromell, N. (2004) Children's fitness testing: Feasibility study commissioned by the National Assembly for Wales. Loughborough: School of Sport and Exercise Sciences.

Houlihan, B. (2002) 'Sporting excellence, school and sports development: The politics of crowded policy spaces', *European Physical Education Review* Vol. 6, No. 2: pp. 171–194.

Houlihan, B. & White, A. (2002) *The politics of sports development: Development of sport or development through sport?*. London: Routledge.

Humberstone, B. (1990) 'Warriors or wimps? Creating alternative forms of physical education', pp. 201–210 in Messner, M.A. & Sabo, D.F. (eds) *Sport, men and the gender order: Critical feminist perspectives.* Champaign. Ill.: Human Kinetics.

Kinchin, G.D. and O'Sullivan, M. (2003) 'Incidences of student support for and resistance to a curricular innovation in high school physical education', *Journal of Teaching in Physical Education* Vol. 22, No. 3: pp. 245–260.

Kirk, D. (1999a),Physical Culture, Physical Education and Relational Analysis', *Sport, Education and Society* Vol. 4, No. 1: pp. 63–73.

——— (1999b) 'Embodying the school/ schooling bodies: Physical education as disciplinary technology', pp. 181–196 in Symes, C. and Meadmore, D. (eds) *The extra-ordinary school: Parergonality and pedagogy.* New York: Peter Lang.

——— (1998a) 'Educational reform, physical culture and the crisis of legitimation in physical education', *Discourse: Studies in the Cultural Politics of Education* Vol. 19, No. 1: pp. 101–112.

——— (1998b) *Schooling bodies: School practice and public discourse 1880-1950.* London: Leicester University Press.

——— (1992a) *Defining physical education: The social construction of a school subject in postwar Britain.* London: Falmer.

——— (1992b) 'Physical education, discourse and ideology: Bringing the hidden curriculum into view', *Quest* 44, pp. 35–56.

Kirk, D., Brooker, R. and Braiuka, S. (2000) 'Teaching games for understanding: A situated perspective on student learning', Paper presented to the American Educational Research Association Annual Meeting, New Orleans, April.

Kosma, M., Cardinal, B.J. and Rintala, P. (2002) 'Motivating individuals with disabilities to be physically active', *Quest* Vol. 54, No. 2: pp. 116–132.

Lave, J. (1997) 'The culture of acquisition and the practice of understanding', pp. 17–36 in D. Kirshner and J.A. Whitson (eds) *Situated cognition: Social, semiotic and psychological perspectives*. New Jersey: Erlbaum.

Lave, J. and Wenger, E. (1991) *Situated learning: Legitimate peripheral participation*. New York: Cambridge University Press.

Macdonald, D. (2002) 'Critical pedagogy: What might it look like and why does it matter?', pp. 167–189 in Laker, A. (ed) *The sociology of sport and physical education*. London: Routledge/ Falmer.

Maguire, J. (in press) 'Challenging the sports-industrial complex: Human sciences, advocacy and service', *European Physical Education Review*

Maguire, J. & Young, K. (2002, Eds.) *Theory, sport and society*. Oxford: Elsevier Press.

Marshall, S. J., Biddle, S. J. H., Murdey, I., Gorely, T., & Cameron, N. (2003) 'But what are you doing now? Ecological momentary assessment of sedentary behavior among youth' [abstract], *Medicine and Science in Sport and Exercise* Vol. 35, (No. 5, Suppl.), S180.

Nettleton, B. (1968) 'Homo-sedens Australis', *The Australian Journal of Physical Education* 42, pp. 17–36.

Nilges, L.M. (1998) 'I thought only fairy tales had supernatural power: A radical feminist analysis of Title IX in physical education', *Journal of Teaching in Physical Education* Vol. 17, No. 2: pp. 172–194.

Oliver, K.L. & Lalik, R. (2001) 'The body as curriculum: Learning with adolescent girls', *Journal of Curriculum Studies* Vol. 33, No. 3: pp. 303–333.

Penney, D. (2002, Ed.) *Gender and physical education: Contemporary issues and future directions*. London: Routledge.

Penney, D. and Evans, J. (1999) *Politics, policy and practice in physical education*. London: Spon.

Qualifications Curriculum Authority (1999) *Terminology in physical education*. London: Author.

Renold, E. (1997) 'All they've got on their brains is football': Sport, masculinity and the gendered practices of playground relations', *Sport, Education and Society*. Vol. 2, No. 1: pp. 5–24.

Roberts, K. (1996) 'Young people, schools, sport and government policies', *Sport, Education and Society* Vol. 1, No. 1: pp. 47–58.

Sage, G. (2002) 'Global sport and global mass media', pp. 211–233 in Laker, A. (ed) *The sociology of sport and physical education*. London: Routledge/ Falmer.

Scottish Education Department (1972) *Physical education in secondary schools.* Edinburgh: HMSO.

Shilling, C. (1993) *The body and social theory.* London: Sage.

Siedentop, D. (1994) 'The Sport Education model', pp. 3–16 in Siedentop, D. (ed) *Sport education: Quality PE through positive sport experiences.* Champaign, Ill.: Human Kinetics.

Sport England (2002) www. Sportengland.org., accessed 17/1/2002.

Theberge, N. (1985) 'Towards a feminist alternative to sport as a male preserve' *Quest* 37, pp. 193–202.

Vertinsky, P. A. (1992) 'Reclaiming space, revisioning the body: The quest for gender-sensitive physical education', *Quest* 44, pp. 373–396.

Vescio, J, Taylor, T. and Toohey, K. (1999) 'An exploration of sports participation by girls from non-English speaking backgrounds', *ACHPER Healthy Lifestyles Journal* Vol. 6, No. 2/3: pp. 14–19.

Walker, J.C. (1988) *Louts and legends: Male youth culture in an inner city school.* Sydney: Allen & Unwin.

Williams, A.E. (1985) 'Understanding constraints on innovation in physical education', *Journal of Curriculum Studies* Vol. 17, No. 4: pp. 407–13.

Williams, A. & Bedward, J. (2001) 'Gender, culture and the generation gap: Student and teacher perceptions of aspects of the National Curriculum Physical Education', *Sport, Education and Society* Vol. 6, No. 1: pp. 53–66.

Wright, J. (1997) 'The construction of gendered contexts in single-sex and co-educational physical education classes', *Sport, Education and Society* Vol. 2, No. 1: pp. 55–72.

—————— (1996) 'Mapping the discourses of physical education: Articulating a female tradition', *Journal of Curriculum Studies* Vol. 28, No. 3: pp. 331–351.

Wright, J., Macdonald, D. & Burrows, L. (2004, eds) *Critical inquiry and problem-solving in physical education.* London: Routledge.

Wright, J., Macdonald, D. & Groom, L. (2003) 'Physical activity and young people: Beyond participation', *Sport, Education and Society* Vol. 8, No. 1: pp. 17–34.

Young, I.M. (1980) '"Throwing like a girl": A phenomenology of feminine body comportment, motility and spatiality', *Human Studies* 3: pp. 137–156.

INDIFFERENT, HOSTILE OR EMPOWERED? SCHOOL PHYSICAL EDUCATION AND ACTIVE LEISURE LIFESTYLES FOR GIRLS AND YOUNG WOMEN

Anne Flintoff

Carnegie Faculty of Sport and Education
Leeds Metropolitan University

Introduction

This paper aims to evaluate the role of school PE in helping girls and young women adopt active leisure lifestyles. Whilst education for life-long physical activity involvement has been a long established aim of PE, we have been largely unsuccessful in achieving it, and particularly so for girls and women. New evidence of our unacceptably high levels of inactivity emerge almost daily, with the latest survey from the Department of Health (2004) showing girls having higher levels of inactivity than boys. However, rarely is there any kind of moral panic about the significance of girls' levels of activity compared to boys.

Over the last three decades, feminist researchers have sought to explain these differences as the consequence of complex gender relations that operate to constrain girls' and women's opportunities and experiences. As our understanding of gender relations has become increasingly sophisticated, we have moved from viewing girls and women as a homogeneous group, to recognition of the diversity between them, and the interconnections between gender, sexuality, 'race' and class. Importantly, this work has also shown how gender power relations create hierarchies between boys and men as a group, and how sport and PE operate to construct and celebrate hegemonic forms of masculinities. So whilst the focus of this paper is on girls and young women, it should not be assumed that PE and school sport is unproblematic for at least some boys and some young men too. I will return to this point later in the paper.

There has been a huge level of investment in PE and school sport over recent years, with numerous new policies and initiatives being introduced. One of the latest documents to emerge from the PE and School Sport Clubs Links strategy (PESSCL) national strategy is called High Quality PE and Sport for Young People (DfES/DCMS, 2004). This paper explores what might count as high quality PE and school sport for girls and young women? How do the new initiatives currently being implemented encourage girls and young women to be physically active in their leisure, and what if anything is changing as a result of the new strategy?

Central to the argument presented here is an interrogation over what counts as PE today. As Evans, Davies and Penney (1996) suggest,

> What passes for PE is neither arbitrary nor immutable. It is a social and cultural construct, laden with values which not all would adhere to or want to share. PE ... consequently makes both friends and enemies of those subjected to it, it inspires and it alienates, it conditions and reconditions class and cultural (gender, ability and 'race') subjectivities, power relations and structures. (Evans, Davies and Penney, 1996: p. 167)

Historical accounts of the development of PE show the social construction of PE as a school subject to be characterised by two gendered, sub-cultures, each with different ideas about how and what PE should be (Fletcher, 1984). However, I argue that contemporary PE is now a narrow, masculinized, sport-based PE, where competition and performance matter more than children and learning — and in which girls and young women — but also many boys and young men too — struggle to establish a place and identity. In order to understand how we have arrived at this position, the paper begins by briefly exploring the development of girls' PE from early origins over a century ago, and contrasting this with today, where the practices and thinking that have historically characterised men's PE have become dominant in contemporary PE practice. It then goes on to explore the implications of this narrow, sport-based PE for girls and young women, drawing on two qualitative research studies (Flintoff and Scraton, 2001; Flintoff, 2003). Qualitative research offers a counter to the much publicised quantitative surveys of young people and their activity rates that show girls and young women as 'problems' for their under representation (e.g. Sport England, 2003). The first study sought to explore the meaning and place of physical activity in the lives of young women, and the links — if any — between school PE and out of school physical activity involvement (see Flintoff and Scraton, 2001). The second research study is beginning to evaluate the School Sport Coordinator programme, a key aspect of the national PESSCL strategy. This programme is particularly interesting here, since it has the specific aim of encouraging life long active leisure, and linking curriculum PE with out-of-school sporting opportunities and pathways, particularly for girls as one of its target groups. By drawing on findings from both of these studies, the paper aims to demonstrate the huge gap between the experiences and aspirations of many young women and what is provided in contemporary PE and sport practice.

The female tradition in PE

How has girls' PE developed from its earlier origins to the sport-based PE of today? Fletcher (1984) documents how the beginning of girls' PE began with the training of specialised women PE teachers in the late nineteenth century, in separate colleges, with a distinctive 'female tradition' and culture (Fletcher, 1984). It was only much later that the first training college for men PE teachers opened at Carnegie in Leeds in 1933. Women's PE teacher training emphasised the importance of physical activity for women's health and well-being, and incorporated a child-centred approach, drawing on a broad range of physical activities including dance, gymnastics and some games. As Kirk (1992) has shown in his historical research on men's PE, the male tradition was quite different, growing out of different roots, and influenced by militarism and competitive team games. Whilst I argue that today's PE is a masculinized, sport-based PE, it is important to stress that the early beginning of girls' PE were not devoid of gendered assumptions and ideologies either. Girls' PE was underpinned by powerful images and ideas about women, their roles and capabilities. Callisthenics, and the later introduction of Ling gymnastics were seen as gentle, appropriate exercise for girls' health and wellbeing (Fletcher, 1984). The women's PE colleges were influential in developing a comprehensive and balanced PE, and underpinning the teaching was an educational philosophy that centred on the development of self-control; neatness; service to others; discipline and respect for authority. These became the 'standards' of girls' PE, and formed the basis of both medical and educational inspections of the subject at the time. So whilst the development of separate training for women PE teachers challenged some gendered expectations of women's physical capabilities by giving them access to sport and physical activities previously denied to them, this separate tradition was also underpinned by powerful gendered ideologies of femininity and physicality that influenced and shaped a separate girls' PE curriculum.

An uneasy alliance?

If women had substantially defined what was understood as PE until the 1950s, from the 1960s onwards, Fletcher (1984) argues that this position was consistently eroded. A number of factors were involved here, not least, the closing of many of the specialist PE colleges, or their merger with institutions of higher education in the 1970s, and the push to develop 'degree-worthiness' in the subject. She and others conclude that it was a narrowly masculinized form of sport-based PE that became established over this period (Fletcher, 1984; Kirk, 1992; 2002). However, as Kirk (2002) reminds us, it is important to note that 'the male version of PE is not a totalised discourse', nor for that matter, should it be assumed that there was a total homogeneity amongst the values and dispositions of male or female professionals within the separate spheres of male and female PE. So whilst PE did shift towards a male definition of PE, there were always spaces for teachers to practice alternative forms to the dominant discourse. And this was the case during the late 1970s and early 1980s — a significant time in the social construction of PE, and where a number of new practices emerged, to become known as the 'New PE' (Evans, 1990). Reflecting the broader educational discourse of equal opportunities at the time, innovations such as Teaching Games for Under-standing and Health Related Fitness initiatives provided a challenge to conventional PE practice, particularly the emphasis on competitive team games and its authoritarian pedagogical modes (Evans and Clarke, 1988). Both initiatives were child-centred, rather than subject centred, and focused on less didactive modes of teaching, and as Evans and Clarke (1988) conclude, this was not so much 'new' PE at all, but in some respects PE that reflected the traditions of girls' PE.

In addition to these initiatives, there was also discussion and action around equal opportunities in PE, specifically in relation to access of girls (and sometimes boys) to different curriculum activities, and to single sex and co-educational teaching (Leaman, 1984; ILEA, 1984; *British Journal of Physical Education*, 1987). Although drawing on the traditions of liberal feminism, these initiatives were important for challenging the sex-differentiated curriculum, sex stereotyping by teachers, and improving girls' access and opportunities. However, whilst the discourse of New PE did challenge aspects of traditional practice, it always remained a marginal discourse and one with which many PE teachers failed to engage voluntarily. Many schools, for example, introduced mixed PE as a result of a shortage of resources, rather than any ideological commitment to equal opportunities (Evans, *et al.*, 1985; Scraton, 1993).

By the late 1980s, any excitement and enthusiasm created by the New PE had largely been destroyed by the concerted attacks launched more broadly on the education profession and on PE within it. By 1988, the new Right's conservative ideologies had become firmly embedded in the education system through the passing of the Education Reform Act (ERA). With ERA came a whole raft of complex and interlocking changes; more accountability for schools; a market philosophy that set schools in competition with one another, and importantly for this discussion, including the introduction of a national curriculum in PE (NCPE).

Extensive research by Evans and Penney (1999) has detailed the complex ways in which the process of defining the first NCPE, implemented from 1992, unfolded, showing the influence of dominant discourses and contexts outside of education, most notably of sport, on the finalised school version (Evans and Penney, 1995). Drawing on the work of Stephen Ball (1990) they show how the making of the NCPE reflected a struggle over competing discourses, in particular, between what Ball has called the discourses of 'progressivism' and 'cultural restoration'.

The Education Reform Act and after

A progressive discourse of schooling emphasises the child, the skills and processes of learning and problem solving pedagogies. In contrast, exponents of cultural restoration argue for a return to pre-comprehensivization ideals — for an ability-differentiated system of education, a discrete subject based curriculum, and for a pedagogy of systematic transmission. It was this latter discourse, cultural restoration, which became more powerful, and despite the struggles inherent in its making, as Evans and Penney (1995) show, it was the characteristics of men's PE that articulated with such a discourse, and that became central to the NCPE.

The NCPE became a curriculum constructed around discrete activity areas — games, gymnastics, dance and so on–with an emphasis on skill acquisition and performing, and a privileging of games over other programmes of study. The broad, balanced curriculum initially proposed was dismissed by the Secretary of State in the interests of providing 'flexibility' for schools, but significantly that flexibility did not extend to games which were made compulsory for all children up to the age of fourteen! In so doing, the NCPE became a curriculum that centralised the sport discourse of a traditionally male conception of PE. As Penney (2002) argues, through the privileging of games, the flexibility in the policy, and the silences and omissions around issues of equity, the NCPE was an implicitly gendered text. In particular, it specifically allowed for the continuation of sex-stereotyped pattern of games provision where different games are taught to girls and boys, with female and male teachers delivering each respectively. And as Hargreaves (2000: p. 140) has noted, "it is the 'hidden curriculum' of competitive team games, more than any other aspect of the PE curriculum, that replicates conventional notions of gender difference".

Since then, of course, there have been numerous pressures and incentives for teachers to adopt practices that further entrench a sport-based PE. The rapid growth and increasing influence of the Youth Sport Trust has seen its many sport-based initiatives become firmly embedded within PE and school sport programmes. Similarly, although the NCPE has been revised twice, the current version has seen minimal change; a bit more autonomy for teachers to select activities other than games at Key Stage 4, and the call for teachers to pay 'due regard' in their teaching to three principles for inclusion (Penney, 2002). However, teachers are given no guidance about how they might work to these principles, and to date, inclusion has largely been interpreted in terms of ability, with a focus on the inclusion of children with special educational needs or with exceptional talent (Bailey and Morley, 2003; Vickerman, 2003). Discourses of gender equity, if they ever had more than a shaky foothold on the educational agenda, are now very much absent, and particularly so in PE.

Girls' PE has come a long way from its early origins, as a separate sphere of influence, developed and controlled by women for women, to the narrow, masculinized, sport-based version controlled largely by men[1] that characterises contemporary PE practice. However, there is a danger that by focusing on the changing nature of the subject content of PE, that we lose sight of how PE gets delivered, and importantly, how it is experienced by youngsters. The form and processes of PE are important if we are to understand what young people learn in PE.

The next section of the paper considers how young women are experiencing PE today. During the 1990s feminist theorising in education has shifted away from the structural analysis of shared oppression to focus on difference and diversity, emphasizing the pluralities of femininities and girls' experiences, as well as masculinities and boys' experiences. Post structural analyses focusing on language and discourse have offered new insights into our understanding of gender (in PE, see Wright's work, 1996; 1997); however, they have also been criticised for ignoring the material realities of young women's lives (Scraton, 1993). In a study of young people that explored the links between PE and physical activity involvement out of school, as well as addressing some of these theoretical concerns, we attempted to explore the interface between micro and macro, between individual women's identities and the broader social structures and cultural settings in which they exist (Flintoff & Scraton, 2001).

Young women and active lifestyles

Group and individual interviews with young women revealed the very varied meaning and place of physical activity in their lives. Many were active, although in very different activities, with different levels of engagement and commitment. This ranged from Helen[2], for example, who danced four times a week, in addition to taking GCSE dance (all out of school because dance was not on offer within the curriculum), to others who went for an occasional jog round the park.

For most, there was little or no link between school based activities, and those engaged in out of school settings. The few young women who were committed to competitive team games were very much the exception. More usually, school PE activities were viewed as 'babyish' and old fashioned. It is important to stress here that the four schools all had committed and hard working teachers trying to meet the needs of their young people, and offered a wide range of activities at Key Stage 4, with some choice. Whilst appreciated, many of the young women were keen to point out that this did not always offer them a 'real' choice because of the context and environment in which these were on offer. If offered in mixed groupings, activities like football or basketball were avoided since this often meant marginalisation or ridicule by the boys or over zealous competition, not dealt with by the teachers. Several young women commented that they felt that their teachers expected them to be reluctant participants. One school had reverted back to single sex PE for all their lessons, and had also allowed pupils a say in the clothing they wore for PE, both strategies that resulted from young women's resistance to existing practices. These findings are, disturbingly, nothing new. So little seems to have changed since Scraton carried out her major study of girls' PE in the late 1980s (Scraton, 1992). Many female PE teachers continue to see the traditional PE kit (for girls, usually a short skirt, tee shirt and PE knickers) as important for maintaining standards and projecting a 'respectable' female image. Young women's perceptions, however, are quite different as Anne's comment here reveals:

> ["What do you wear for PE?"]

> "... something ridiculous and awful! It's one of my real hates! For trampolining we are allowed to wear LEGGINGS, but is kind of purvy ... like before we started complaining at the Student Council, they would go you MUST wear a gym skirt and you MUST wear knickers under that, and we would say excuse me! I mean does the uniform have any effect on my performance in PE, I don't see the point of it. We can now wear shorts, because we complained, or leggings or tracksuit bottoms." [*Anne, School 3, group interview*]

On one hand its revealing nature potentially puts their bodies on display and open to unwanted heterosexual male gaze and comment; on the other, it is viewed as childish and incompatible with their developing adult heterosexual femininity.

The research revealed significant differences between the young women's attitudes to PE in different schools, suggesting that pedagogical practices of individual teachers do make a difference. Some teachers had clearly been able to work with some of the young women in ways that were empowering — for example, allowing them to bring in their own music, giving them more control over the content of the lessons, and importantly, using pedagogies and learning activities that were inclusive of different abilities.

The young women were very much aware of gender relations and the contradictions and ambiguities raised for them, and were also resigned to the fact that teachers would do little to challenge things like dominant boys' behaviours in mixed groups. In contrast to their experiences in school, many of the young women were active in out of school settings that seemed to be less gendered. These were often single sex, and contexts where they could choose their level of commitment and involvement. However, physical activity involvement in out of school contexts involved weighing up the relative costs, and negotiating hurdles and barriers too. The costs of activities, travelling to and from venues, and having someone to go with were all significant, as well as finding a sympathetic coach or leader that would help them develop their skills.

Our study reveals the range of subject positions young women adopt in relation to physical activity. Many young women want to be, and are active, but this appears to be despite their PE in schools, rather than as a result of it. The young women in our study were largely indifferent to PE and struggled to see its purpose, some were more hostile to it, actively choosing not to engage by forgetting their kit or skipping school, and only a minority, such as Rebecca, very committed to hockey, had experienced it as positive and empowering. Physical activity involvement remained largely contingent on them successfully managing and negotiating a number of hurdles, including the impact of gender relations.

Even the 'performance pathways' in competitive sport are not so clear for young women. The few young women in our study who were committed to traditional competitive team sport, found they were too old to play for school-based teams, but felt 'too young' at 15 years, to join an adult club; as a result, several had stopped their participation altogether. For Rebecca, a talented hockey player, it was easier: with middle class, supportive parents, and a high level of talent, her transition to club hockey was relatively straightforward. However, many clubs — like school PE — do not cater well for youngsters of different abilities.

One of the weaknesses of our study was the lack of minority ethnic young women we were able to talk to. Despite a head of girls' PE admitting to us on our first meeting that 'she had real trouble with the Asian girls', none were included in the pupils who volunteered to talk to us. As a result, our study cannot say much about the experiences of minority ethnic women, or how racialised aspects of gender relations might impact on this, although comments such as the head of department's suggest that this remains an important area for future research (but see Benn, 1996; 2002; Wray, 2002). However, our study does show that young women's physical activity involvement cannot be divorced from an understanding of the complexities of their developing femininities and lives as young women, and the wider structural and institutional contexts of physical activity opportunities.

The School Sport Coordinator Programme

I now turn to one of the newer policies within the national PE and school sport strategy, the School Sport Coordinator Programme. A central aim of this programme is the strategic development of partnerships to improve both the quality and opportunities for PE and youth sport.

Diagram 1 shows one of the school sport partnerships, centred on a family of schools. The programme revolves around school sport partnerships, at the hub of which is a sport college — a state secondary school specialising

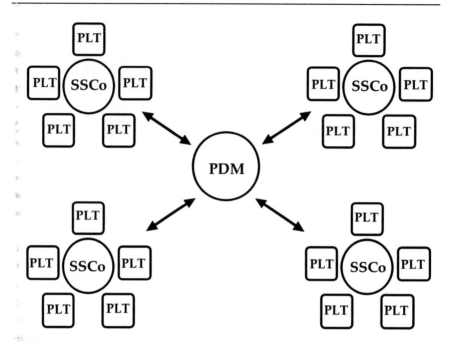

Diagram 1   *Preferred partnership model*

in PE and sport, with a partnership development manager (PDM) (normally an experienced PE teacher managing its development. The PDM works with a sport coordinator, a PE teacher released from teaching for two days a week to undertake development work in each of their surrounding secondary schools and each of these work with a Primary Link Teacher, a teacher in their feeder primary schools. Working as a partnership, the aim of the programme is to build links and networks between these schools, and between the schools and outside agencies offering physical activities for young people.

There are a lot of positive features about the School Sport Coordinator (SSCo) programme for helping young people adopt active leisure lifestyles — firstly, the programme is built around local partnerships in local contexts. Secondly, PE teachers, who work with young people every day, are driving the programme, ensuring that activities are appropriate and educational in the broadest sense (one of the aims of the programme is that it contributes to youngsters' wider educational development, not just sport). And lastly, a key aim of the programme is to increase the activity levels of previously under represented groups with girls and young women as one of these.

So how is this programme working in practice? I will draw here on some of the findings of an ongoing study of one partnership in the north of England that I have called 'Northbridge' (Flintoff, 2003). Through observation and in depth interviewing with key personnel in the programme, we have been interested in exploring the ways in which the policy is embedding into practice across this partnership in its first, three-year phase. Here I have only space to draw out a few aspects of the research relating to the delivery of the programme, and teachers' perceptions of targeting, and working with girls and young women. Again, it is important to stress that the teachers in the partnership are all committed individuals, working hard to develop the programme, and the partnership is seen by many in the local authority as one of the more successful.

As Houlihan (2000: p. 181) reminds us, no new policy is introduced into a neutral space; rather in terms of PE and sport, it is into one that 'may not only be crowded but which already possesses a pattern of power relations established as a result of an earlier policy'. In the case of the SSCo programme, the policy context of PE and sport is one in which a sport-based national curriculum, supported by an extra curricular programme of inter-school team competition, has been firmly established, particularly in the secondary schools (Penney and Harris, 1997). This existing policy agenda has acted as a major limitation on the range of activities and physical activity opportunities offered as part of the programme at Northbridge.

To support the development of 'quality PE', the school sports coordinators' (SSCos) natural starting point is to do more of the activities that form the NCPE. The result is that the hegemony of competitive sport within the curriculum gets replicated in the out of school hours learning opportunities developed by the programme. This trend is exacerbated by the skills and interests of the individual SSCos. At all but one of the SSCos are male, secondary trained PE teachers, and admit to having lower levels of skills and interest in the areas of dance and gymnastics, compared to team games. 'Ossie', for example, admitted that in his first year as a SSCo, he wanted to 'lead by example', and as he was qualified and interested in soccer, cricket and basketball, these were the activities he prioritised in his early work with primary schools where he took a very hands on role, delivering most of the sessions himself. His enthusiasm and commitment to the role was unquestionable, as is the increase in opportunities for sport that have resulted from his work. But by his own admission, as the quote below suggests, he felt it was a too much to a challenge to engage youngsters (girls or boys!) that were not interested in these sports:

"... anyone who wants to come can play. There are three categories aren't there? there are the kids that have elite talent, and represent school teams, kids that aren't good enough to take part in school teams and then those that don't want to participate ... .can we capture any of the last group? Not yet, think that you would have to start with the first two and once you have got them in place ... . It would be too ambitious to try and reach that third category." [*Ossie, SSCo*]

Targeting under represented groups for Ossie has entailed ensuring his games activities have been open to boys and girls. Similarly, Neil, in his first year of teaching, is reluctant to provide opportunities that might engage other than 'Mr Average':

"Simply by targeting people, you are excluding people right away though aren't you? I don't think you should exclude people just because they are Mr average, so all the clubs have been open ... The activities we have done tend towards games activities, and now whether that is including or excluding — it is possible that is an issue ... ." [*Neil, SSCo*]

Perhaps more worrying is the way in which the format of selective, competitive team sport — more characteristic of the secondary schools — is being implemented primary schools. Half termly blocks of coaching sessions in NCPE activities have culminated with an inter-school competitive 'festival'. This format means that only a minority of pupils (the high ability pupils) are selected to represent their school team to compete against other schools. One primary link teacher (who was also the head teacher of the school) suggested that the out of school football club had become more serious after entering a team in the local league — and suggested 'although we believe in 100% participation, at the end of the day, we want to win that league'. When probed, she admitted that the team was all boys, and the girls' attendance at the club had dropped off after they had not been selected to play for the team! They had gone to establish a club for girls on another day, so that they 'could develop their skills in order to have the confidence to compete with the boys.' She went on to suggest that it was very difficult to engage some girls, particularly Asian girls, however hard they tried because at the end of the day, it was their choice not to get involved.

The emphasis placed on team sports has also been exacerbated by the difficulties of recruiting coaches to deliver out of school activities. Recruiting coaches in soccer and rugby, or from national governing bodies that have been proactive at targeting schools to talent scout, such as table tennis, has been easier than it is in other activities such as dance or gymnastics. This is despite the sometimes huge efforts some teachers have made to provide an interesting and balanced programme for their pupils. For example, in one school, a teacher was specifically employed to teach Asian dance to encourage participation by the girls. Although very successful, the primary link teacher reluctantly had to admit that she could not afford to extend the programme as the teacher was just too expensive for the group sizes she was able to work with. Coaches from a local professional soccer club on the other hand, came 'free' — their activities forming part of their community outreach programme. Although there had been some concern about the quality and appropriateness of these sessions, for some primary teachers, struggling to do the best for their pupils in PE, with inadequate facilities and resources, and with some hesitancy in their own skills to deliver PE, any coach is considered better than no coach!

It is important to mention examples of good practice in the Northbridge partnership — to give one example, a table tennis coach, whilst clearly having the long-term aim of developing and identifying talent, delivered high quality, differentiated sessions, as well as ensuring teachers had access to in-service training and free equipment, to ensure the sustainability of her sessions. As Kirk and Gorely (2000) have shown, PE and sport should not necessarily be considered mutually exclusive; sport can be used educationally, but requires educated coaches and teachers, able to use modified game forms and child-centred pedagogy, and with more clearly identified participation opportunities, as well as performance pathways.

There is no doubt that the Northbridge partnership is providing more opportunities in and out of the curriculum for children to be active. However, many of these opportunities have been through inter-school competitions in a narrow range of traditional, and often traditionally male, sport. Whilst clearly beneficial to some girls — the girls' cricket and football festivals were deemed successful events — it is evident that the programme is failing to provide for many others. Observations of partnership meetings reveal little evidence of coordinators reflecting on their practice, specifically in relation to moving outside a dominant discourse of sport, or any real consideration of the needs of so-called under represented groups. This is not at all surprising given the policy context in which they are working, and the lack of a strong lead in these issues in the continuing professional development associated with the programme. Girls (and boys) are required to fit into a sport-based PE, orientated towards competition and elite performance, and for the most part, their absence is explained away as the 'natural' reluctance of girls to get involved.

Conclusion

This paper has tried to show how girls' PE has shifted away from its historical, educational roots to the sports based form today, and the implications of this for young women's physical activity involvement. Whilst not wishing to infer that the separate sphere of girls' PE was unproblematic, it is clear that moves to integrate the two traditions of PE has resulted in a masculinized model becoming dominant. It is also clear that this masculinized model is one built on a particularly narrow version of masculinity that has implications for boys and young men too. Although there is no space here to explore the data gathered from the young men in our young people study, many of them, too, struggled to find a place and identity (see Bramham, 2003). Sport-based PE not just reinforces gender difference, but also reinforces hierarchical forms of masculinity. By exploring young women's qualitative experiences of PE and physical activity, we can begin to appreciate why many of them choose to 'drop out' of active leisure. Indeed, we might be surprised at how many manage to maintain a physical activity involvement, given the hurdles they have to negotiate. It is clear from our initial research findings that the new policies, such as the school sport coordinator programme, are doing little to address these, or challenge the hegemony of sport-based provision for young people.

Can we really claim we are currently providing high quality PE and sport for girls and young women? I suspect not. I am pessimistic about how things might change, but at the centre of that change must be a critical analysis of contemporary PE discourse, and a reinsertion of a critical gendered analysis. This has to be one that goes beyond a simplistic view of gender that sees boys and girls as homogeneous categories, towards a consideration of how different forms of femininity and masculinity are produced and reproduced through PE and youth sport. In particular, we need more work that critically evaluates the form and processes of boys' PE and the ways in which sport-based PE reinforces hegemonic forms of masculinity (see Bramham, 2003). We need also to return to an educational discourse in PE, where we focus on what and how young people learn in and through PE, and where we provide a physical education for leisure, rather than simply, sport as leisure.

Notes

1 We urgently need research that builds on and updates the work of Sikes (1988) and which seeks to explore the relationships between contemporary conceptions of PE and school sport and gendered career progressions. The statistics available suggest that men continue to hold the majority of decision making positions within contemporary PE: for example, 75% of the heads of PE and sport in the new sports colleges are men (see Penney, Houlihan and Ely, 2002).

2 All names are pseudonyms.

References

Ball, S.J. (1990) *Politics and policy making in education*. London: Routledge.

Benn, T. (1996) 'Muslim women and physical education in initial teacher training', *Sport, Education and Society* Vol. 1, No. 1: pp. 5–21.

Benn, T. (2002) 'Muslim women in teacher training: Issues of gender, 'race' and religion', in D. Penney (ed) *Gender and Physical Education: Contemporary issues and future directions*. London: Routledge.

Bramham, P. (2003) 'Boys, masculinity and PE', *Sport, Education and Society* Vol. 8, No. 1: pp. 57–71.

British Journal of Physical Education (1987)

David, M. E. (1993) 'Parents, gender, and education', *Educational Policy* Vol. 7, No. 2: p. 184.

Davies, B., Evans, J., Penney, D., & Bass, D. (1997) 'Physical education and nationalism in Wales', *Curriculum Journal* Vol. 8, No. 2: pp. 249–270.

De Knop, P., Theeboom, M., Wittock, H., & De Martelaer, K. (1996) 'Implications of Islam on Muslim girls' sports participation in Western Europe', Literature review and policy recommendations for sport promotion. *Sport, Education and Society* Vol. 1, No. 2: pp. 147–164.

Department for Education and Skills/Department for Culture, Media and Sport 2004. *High quality PE and sport for young people*. Annsely: DfES publications.

Department of Health (2004) *At least five a week: Evidence on the impact of physical activity and its relationship to health*. London: Crown.

Ennis, C. D. (1999) 'Creating a culturally relevant curriculum for disengaged girls', *Sport Education and Society* Vol. 4, No. 1: pp. 31–50.

Evans, J. (1990) 'Defining a subject: The rise and fall of the new PE', *British Journal of Sociology of Education* Vol. 11, No. 2: pp. 155–169.

Evans, J., & Clarke, G. (1988) 'Changing the face of physical education', in J. Evans (ed) *Teachers, teaching — and control in physical education*. London: Falmer.

Evans, J., Davies, B., & Penney, D. (1996) 'Teachers, teaching and the social construction of gender relations', *Sport, Education and Society* Vol. 1, No. 2: pp. 165–183.

Evans, J., Lopez, S., Duncan, M., & Evans, M. (1985) 'Some thoughts on the political and pedagogical implications of mixed sex PE grouping in the PE curriculum', *British Educational Research Journal*, 13(1), 59–71.

Evans, J. & Penney, D. (1995) 'The politics of pedagogy: Making a National Curriculum Physical Education', *Journal of Education Policy* Vol. 10, No. 1: pp. 27.

Evans, J. & Williams, T. (1989) 'Moving up and getting out: The classed and gendered career opportunities of physical education teachers', in T. Templin & P. Schempp (eds) *Socialisation into Physical Education: Learning to Teach*. Carmel: Benchmark Press.

Fletcher, S. (1984) *Women first: The female tradition in English physical education, 1880–1980*. London: Athlone.

Flintoff, A. (2003) 'The School Sport Co-ordinator Programme: Changing the role of the physical education teacher?', *Sport Education and Society* Vol. 8, No. 2: pp. 231–250.

Flintoff, A., & Cooke, B. (2002) 'An evaluation of an out of school hours learning in PE and sport programme: Interim report Feb 2002', *Bulletin of Physical Education* Vol. 38, No. 2: pp. 99–110.

Flintoff, A., & Scraton, S. (2001) 'Stepping into active leisure? Young women's perceptions of active lifestyles and their experiences of school physical education', *Sport Education and Society* Vol. 6, No. 1: pp. 5–22.

Fox, K., & Harris, J. (2003) 'Promoting physical activity through schools', in J. McKenna & C. Riddoch (eds) *Perspectives on health and exercise*. Basingstoke: Palgrave Macmillan.

Hargreaves, J. (1994) *Sporting females: Critical issues in the history and sociology of women's sports*. London: Routledge.

———— (2000) *Heroines of sport: The politics of difference and identity*. New York: Routledge.

Houlihan, B. (2000) 'Sporting excellence, schools and sports development: The politics of crowded policy spaces', *European Physical Education Review* Vol. 6, No. 2: pp. 171–193.

Inner London Education Authority 1984. *Providing equal opportunities for girls and boys in physical education.* London: Inner London Education Authority College of Physical Education.

Kirk, D. (1992) *Defining physical education: The social construction of a subject in postwar britain.* Basingstoke: Falmer Press.

Kirk, D. (2002) 'Physical Education: A gendered history', in D. Penney (ed) *Gender and Physical Education: Contemporary Issues and future directions.* London: Falmer.

Leaman, O. (1984) *Sit on the sidelines and watch the boys play: Sex differentiation in physical education.* London: Longman for Schools Council.

Penney, D. (2002) 'Gendered policies', in D. Penney (ed) *Gender and physical education: Contemporary issues and future directions.* London: Routledge.

Penney, D., & Evans, J. (1999) *Politics, policy and practice in physical education.* London: E and F N Spon.

Penney, D., & Harris, J. (1997) 'Extra-curricular physical education: More of the same for the more able', *Sport Education and Society* Vol. 2, No. 1: pp. 41–54.

Penney, D., Houlihan, B., & Ely, D. (2002) *Specialist sports colleges national monitoring and evaluation research project: First national survey report.* Unpublished manuscript, Institute of Youth Sport: Loughborough University,.

Scraton, S. (1992) *Shaping up to womanhood: Gender and girls' physical education.* Buckingham: Open University Press.

——— (1993) 'Equality, co-education and physical education in secondary schooling', in J. Evans (ed) *Equality, Education and Physical Education.* London: Falmer.

——— (1994) 'The changing world of women and leisure: Feminism, 'postfeminism' and leisure', *Leisure Studies* Vol. 13, No. 4: pp. 249–262.

Sikes, P. (1988) 'Growing old gracefully? Age, identity and physical education', in J. Evans (ed) *Teachers , teaching — and control in — physical education.* Lewes: Falmer.

Sport England (2003) *Young people and sport in England: Trends in Participation 1994–2002.* London: Sport England.

Wright, J. (1996) 'The construction of complementarity in physical education', *Gender and Education, 8*(1), 61–79.

Wright, J. (1997) 'The construction of gender contexts in single sex and co-educational physical education lessons', *Sport, Education and Society* Vol. 2, No. 1: pp. 55–72.

EXTREME SPORTS AND NATIONAL SPORT POLICY IN CANADA

Joanne Kay
Sport Canada

Purpose

The purpose of this paper is, first, to explore the potential of public investment in extreme sport as a strategy to enhance youth sport participation in Canada and, second, to evaluate the usefulness of a social capital approach to policy analysis. As further work will need to be done in this area, the intention of this paper is to draft a framework for continuing analysis.

Background

The Canadian Sport Policy

Canada has a decentralized sport system with responsibilities distributed amongst the provincial/territorial, national and community levels. The Canadian Sport Policy is the product of extensive collaboration between 14 government jurisdictions, the Canadian sport community and other stakeholders, and it centers on shared goals to enhance participation, excellence, capacity and interaction in the sport system.

The Canadian Sport Policy goal for enhanced participation is to increase sport and physical activity levels by 10% in each province and territory by 2010 when Canada hosts the winter Olympics. As growing evidence demonstrates that Canadian young people are among the least active in the world, children and youth have been identified as priority groups.

Sport as social driver

Many governments (e.g. Canada, UK) have expanded their traditional focus on high-performance to address sport's contribution to other social policy priorities such as health and social cohesion. Sport participation is decreasingly viewed as simply a leisure activity; it is increasingly recognized as a social driver, supporting the development and welfare of individuals, specifically youth.

While the social impacts, benefits (and limitations) of organized sport for youth are becoming better evidenced; the impact of youth participation in *unorganized* sport is coming into focus as well. New research, funded by the Canadian Population Health Initiative, part of the Canadian Institute for Health Information, found that kids who play sport are less likely to be overweight, and that the most profound protective effect came from unorganized sports — activities such as road hockey (Tremblay and Willms, 2003). Accordingly, kids 'playing in the street' spend more hours on the move than those in sport leagues. The co-authors suggested further that funding organized sport did little to address the obesity problem in Canada (which tripled in the country between 1981 and 1996) as it continues to reach the middle and upper socioeconomic-status families — those who are already at a lower risk of having obese children in the first place. A recent British study by Chris Gratton (2004) similarly concluded: "policy intervention, to increase participation, needs to be concentrated in the non-competitive, informal area of sport participation since this is where it is more likely to attract the groups that will yield the highest health benefits from participation."

Current government of Canada sport support

The Government of Canada (Sport Canada) currently contributes to the growth of sport participation by funding sports that meet the following definition:

> Sport is a regulated form of physical activity organized as a contest between two or more participants for the purpose of determining a winner by fair and ethical means. Sport is governed by and sanctioned by a sport federation that holds responsibility for, notably, setting out the rules of play, for awarding champion-ships, and designating the winners of its championships. Further, Sport Canada has established that a sport should meet the

following set of characteristics:

- Its primary activity involves physical interaction between participants and/or between participants and the environment
- It requires specialized neuromuscular skills that involve large muscle groups and which can be taught, learned and improved
- It relies on recognized general principles of long term athlete development
- It involves formal rules and procedures
- It requires fair, ethical and effective tactics and strategies
- It requires a competitive format and structure
- Its competitive events require the on site presence of sanctioned officials.

Currently, like most alternative sports, few extreme sports — especially those in developmental phases — can meet funding eligibility requirements and therefore access sport participation development funds according to current guidelines. From an operational standpoint (as well as a sociological standpoint to be developed in this paper), Sport Canada — Non-Governmental Organization (NGO) — private sector partnerships, such as those currently being explored by Sport Canada, offer the most potentially valuable opportunity for increasing youth sport participation in extreme sports.

Changing environments for sport policy makers

Transformations in the 'field' of sport

Because most government sport policies are rooted in an operational model developed in the 1960's, it has been difficult to address emergent sport practice through policy or programs. Consequently, social and cultural policy makers have largely ignored the popularization of extreme sports. In the 1980s, sport underwent major transformations in technical and technological innovations through creativity and science. The media-sport relationship intensified, sport matured as a distinct economic sector, and sport experienced contemporary ('postmodern') transformation in its values and symbols.

Often characterized as alternative or even counter-cultural, 'extreme' — or 'lifestyle', or 'action' — sports are said to have emerged out of the cultural revolution that took place in the 1950s and 1960s in the United States after the Second World War, when the economy grew more dependent on mass production and mass consumption. A counterculture developed in response to American conformist materialism (exemplified by the Beatnik movement that took place in San Francisco). Youth rejected the rules of social organization and promoted values linked to individual expression and nature, values that implied opposition to a destructive industrial society. The new extreme movement in sport was part of a larger system of opposition and criticism — most often associated with postmodernity — taking place in other domains like music, art, literature and film.

The extreme movement has been traced to surfing- considered to be a marginal and socially rebellious lifestyle based on the rejection of American consumption. Surfers were perhaps the first athletes in the history of modern sport to use sport in the perspective of social marginalization rather than social integration.

Although the anti-mainstream — or marginal — image of extreme sports is still apparent, much of the opposition has largely been eroded or transformed. Its relationship with media and corporate sponsors, for example, has de-emphasized — or even reversed — the oppositional ideology that fueled its earlier motivation. They currently enjoy a paradoxical status as mediatized and corporatized practices still, however, characterized by the rejection of 'mainstream' — or traditional — rules, regulations and conformity. Extreme sports have most recently been described, not in terms of larger political opposition, but as those sports that either ideologically or practically provide alternatives to mainstream sport and to mainstream sport values (Rinehart, Wheaton, Beal, Midol et al). In this sense, they still provide an avenue for youth to use sport in the perspective of social marginalization.

For the purposes of this discussion, we are most interested in those alternative sport practices most popular among youth. Some of these sports are: skateboarding, BMX, aggressive and vertical in-line, street luge, and so on.

Over the past 20 years, there has been a proliferation of these predominantly individualistic new sporting forms, which have resisted institutionalization. The main characteristics of these sports have been described as: risky, innovative, personal, fun, inclusive, participatory and spontaneous. In the twenty-first century, these sports are attracting an ever-increasing number of youth participants, representing a wide range of experiences and levels of involvement. In practical terms, therefore, these activities represent avenues for sporting participation and social engagement for youth who have been alienated by traditional school-based and institutional sport practices (Wheaton).

The 15th annual SUPERSTUDY of Sport Participation, conducted by American Sports Data, Inc (ASD) for the Sporting Goods Manufacturers Association (SGMA) reveals that between 1998 and 2001, the major gains in sports participation have occurred in the 'extreme' sports category. Skateboarding registered a 73% increase, artificial rock climbing increased 57%, wakeboarding 38%, and snowboarding 25%. At the same time, baseball is down 7% and basketball 9%. The trend is largely explained by the propensity of 'Generation Y' for risk-taking.

Bourdieu: framework for analysis

Pierre Bourdieu (1984) provides us with some specific theoretical concepts that can be usefully applied as a framework for analyzing this changing environment for policy makers. Bourdieu is well known for his focus on the symbolic dimension of social life. One of Bourdieu's central claims is that we consume not products but symbols with the intention of establishing social differentiation. Accordingly, it matters little whether individuals prefer one sport to another; what matters is that their preferences express systematic differentiation to those of other groups. Bourdieu therefore highlights sport as a bearer of particular symbolic value — and thus, as a social group signifier — revealing the critical role played by sport practices in the construction/ affirmation of individuals' identity and difference. What is of key importance, therefore, is the recognition that sport choices are fundamentally social rather than being the result of natural disposition or psychological trait.

So how do we choose sport practices? According to Bourdieu, our *habitus* — shaped by socialization and our position in the social structure — mediates between our social position and practice by helping us classify (judge) practices. Through the habitus, we translate our social positions into practices and give meaning to them. In other words, we express our habitus through taste for cultural practice, as our habitus takes into account the *individual* 'social profits' (consciously or unconsciously) expected from sport.

Further, for Bourdieu (1993), cultural practice emerges not simply from habitus, but from the encounter of habitus with *fields* — social arena in which people compete for power or *capital*. One of Pierre Bourdieu's major innovations is the recognition that many forms of capital exist in social life. Cultural capital, social capital, economic capital and physical capital, for example, are all different forms of power, but they share the same level of importance. Accordingly, positions in a field are determined by the unequal distribution of capital and not by the personal attributes of the people in those positions.

Applied to the current problematic, Bourdieu's concepts highlight some specific characteristics of youth participation in extreme sport, such as:

• Because sport is a bearer of particular symbolic value and a social group signifier, youth don't simply choose, for example, between soccer and skateboarding; they choose between the consumption of all lifestyle symbols. Further, the notion of sport as a social group signifier implies that youths interested in extreme sports are most often choosing the sport practices precisely because of — not despite — their marginal position in the field of sport.

• The field of extreme sports is defined *in relation* to the field of mainstream sport. While extreme sports share with mainstream sport media and corporate involvement, they reject institutionalization, quantification and regulation. Accordingly, the forms of symbolic capital efficacious in the field of extreme sports are different from those at play in the field of traditional sport. Participants in extreme sports, for example, are more often concerned with demonstrating creativity and mentorship than quantifiable progression.

• The exclusion of outsiders from groups on the basis of social differentiation illustrates the underpinning of social capital in networks of social relationships. It also underlines the view that social capital can exist in different forms in different networks, and that a form of capital that has currency in one network might hold no value in another. Accordingly, extreme sport can be simultaneously a space of social marginalization, social cohesion and social exclusion.

Social capital: bridging sociology and policy

Pierre Bourdieu's concepts, including social capital, have already proven useful as heuristical devices for investigating the field of sport supply. More recently, the concept of social capital has been explored as a public policy tool. There is a new focus within governments on social capital — understood roughly as networks of social relationships and the resources they embody. From a policy perspective, these networks can be invested in and drawn upon to facilitate action, and can be beneficial as a resource for individuals and communities. In line with Bourdieu's relational theory, policy theorists posit social capital as an approach to investigating social reality that focuses on the relationships among social agents rather than their attributes (Policy Research Initiative 2003)

Although stakeholders debate the relative merits of functional vs. social network approaches and conceptualizations of social capital (individual vs. collective asset, for example), the social capital lens has become valuable for policy makers on two counts: it facilitates categorical understandings of a dynamic social network, and it orients discussions on public policy and action. What is important from a public policy perspective is that social capital is created through the resources and actions of individuals, but its strength (positive or negative) is manifested in its collective social and economic outcomes.

A major step forward in social capital research has been the identification of different forms of social capital. While many categorizations exist, three forms of social capital — bonding, bridging and linking — have been especially helpful in understanding the sources and outcomes of social capital. Bonding social capital refers to relations within homogeneous groups, such as within groups organized around a specific sport practice. Bridging social capital, in contrast, is much more heterogeneous, cutting across diverse social cleavages. This form of social capital is useful in connecting horizontally to external assets and for information diffusion. Linking capital, is similar to bridging capital, but better captures the vertical dimension of social capital. Linking capital refers to ties between different strata of wealth and status –– key to leveraging resources, ideas and information from formal institutions beyond the community.

Implications for policy

For policy makers looking to increase youth sport participation through extreme sports, the central questions from a social capital approach are: (1) should governments be investing in a field of cultural practice marginalizing — and on the margins of — youth engagement? And (2) if so, how should governments invest? From a policy perspective, this first challenge forces examination of cost-benefit. The cost of increasing youth sport participation through investment in extreme sports could be social marginalization of youth and social exclusion among youth. The second challenge suggests the importance of striking an effective but delicate balance between broader public policy goals and specific social group values.

The vision of the Canadian Sport Policy is to create a dynamic and leading edge sport environment that enables *all Canadians* to experience and enjoy involvement in sport to the extent of their abilities and interests. Sport Canada's policies targeting specific groups should therefore aim to ensure that the vision of the Canadian Sport Policy is inclusive, that it has the power to enhance the experience of — and access to — sport for all Canadians equally, including youth disinclined to participate in traditional sport.

Implicit is the recognition that the boundaries of the larger field of sport transcend Sport Canada's current definition of (traditional) sport used for funding eligibility purposes. Also implicit is the recognition that sport 'subfields' exist (i.e. extreme sport, Aboriginal sport practice) — with their own histories, logic and forms of symbolic capital — within the field of sport. The marginal nature of extreme sport participation, which appeals to youth-specific form of social engagement, therefore primarily reflects the diversity and heterogeneity inherent to sport practice. While social exclusion among youth is a downside to this type of sport practice, this is a social issue that transcends participation in extreme sport, indeed, sport generally. From a sociological perspective, social exclusion is a necessary driver of field constituency and cultural identity. Policy can only aim to minimize its negative social impacts, not erase it. An investment in increasing sport participation through extreme sport would therefore not only signal commitment to the vision of the Canadian Sport Policy, but would signal appreciation of the complexity and reality of sport culture.

Responding to the second question — how to invest — is trickier. Appropriating skateboarding within a traditional framework, for example, could disenfranchise youth who participate precisely because of its marginal social signification. To address this question properly, then, the concepts of bonding, bridging and linking should be investigated for their potential value to investment strategies.

By examining bonding, bridging and linking capital within extreme sports, one can appreciate the often paradoxical elements of membership: As defined by bonding capital, extreme sports are spaces of both social exclusion and social cohesion. As defined by bridging capital, extreme sports are paces of brokerage and negotiation with media and corporate agents but are, by design, weak in linking capital, in fact, privileging autonomous, localized power. The challenge, therefore, is to invest in the appropriate forms of social capital to maintain the integrity of the field while reducing barriers to access. This means supporting social cohesion (and tolerating social marginalization) while reducing barriers for excluded groups such as girls. This means exploiting corporate and media ties while preserving field autonomy and agent-deter-mination. And finally, this means driving initiatives from the community level.

The Australian Sports Commission has demonstrated this kind of political flexibility in meeting consumption trends. As an example of a participation strategy, the ASC has partnered with sport organizations and businesses to increase participation in extreme sports. Surfing Australia, the ASC and Coca Cola have announced an investment of $700,000 over the next three years to advance 'Safe Surfing' — a program that helps participants from all backgrounds and with all levels of physical ability to develop surfing skills and knowledge of the environment, first aid, oceanography and surf industry. The ASC has also been ramping up street sports — skateboarding, rollerblading and BMX- with an initiative called "1800 Reverse Street Active." The ASC and several corporate sponsors in partnership with Skate Australia and Freestyle BMX are creating opportunities for children aged 6–15-plus to try a range of street sports. All the equipment is supplied, and coach accreditation courses have been implemented to ensure the health and safety of participants. The group also supports community groups and councils across Australia establishing skate parks and facilities to provide recreational space.

Conclusion

While sport is recognized as a driver for social cohesion and change in Canada, and in the world, the sport solution is most often framed within the context of traditional, state-funded sport. Peter Donnelly and Jay Coakley (2004: 8), in a discussion paper of recreation and youth development, pointed to the emphasis on control and assimilation as problematic: Adult monopoly of power leaves adolescents with a choice between two alternatives — to comply with adult power, or to choose not to participate. An English anecdote from the 1960s is offered to highlight youth autonomy and resistance to adult authority: A group of youths played soccer on a piece of waste ground in Liverpool, using makeshift goals. The municipal recreation department took note and constructed a set of official goals on the site. That night, the youths tore down the goals and continued playing the next day using the broken pieces for their makeshift goals. Donnelly and Coakley (2004: p. 14) noted that a fully democratized form of sport in which the participants determine the form, circumstances and meaning of their participation, might result in the capacity to transform communities: "People could learn initiative, community endeavor, collective rather than individual values, self-determination, etc., that could permit them to take charge of their own lives and communities." Social capital is a resource accumulated by individuals to improve their positions in a social field. The challenge for the policy maker is to determine what forms of social capital underpin a network and how best to utilize this social capital for effective intervention and policy evaluation geared toward the collective good. It is important to note that social capital is not necessarily a positive or collective asset. Critics within Government have cautioned that the view of social capital as a public good tends to emphasize its potentially positive or functional characteristics, while avoiding discussion of its potential downsides. The potential downsides of social capital are associated with the paradoxical capacity of the strong ties and criteria for network membership that are sources of capital, yet which may exclude those who do not meet membership criteria.

For sport policy makers, the extreme sport phenomenon can no longer be ignored as it constitutes a growing field of sport practice specifically suited to youth engagement. While investment strategies must take into account the specific dynamics and forms of capital driving transformations in the field, they must also advance Government of Canada objectives. A primary objective of policy in this area should aim to reduce barriers in the field of extreme sport through community-based private/public partnerships that privilege youth autonomy over government regulation and corporate over government visibility. Effective implantation of relevant policies would achieve the desired outcomes of increased sport participation among youth and youth socialization in view of adult stage (versus immediate) social integration.

References

Bourdieu, P. (1984) *Distinction: A social critique of the judgement of taste.* Trans. Richard Nice. Cambridge: Harvard University Press.

Bourdieu, P. (1993) *Sociology in question.* London: Sage.

Donnelly, P. and Coakley, J. (2004) 'Recreation and youth development: What we know', Paper delivered to the Research Colloquium offered by the Mayor's Panel on Community Safety. Toronto: June 25.

Gratton, C. (2004) 'Sport, health and economic benefit', in Sport England (ed) *Driving up participation: The challenge for Sport England.* London: Sport England.

Policy Research Initiative, Government of Canada (2003) 'Social capital as a public policy development tool', *Horizons* Vol. 6.

Tremblay, M. and Willms, J. D. (2003) 'Is the Canadian childhood obesity epidemic related to physical inactivity?', *International Journal of Obesity* Vol. 27: pp. 1100–5.

THE ROLE OF SPORT FOR YOUNG PEOPLE IN COMMUNITY COHESION AND COMMUNITY SAFETY: ALIENATION, POLICY AND PROVISION

Phil Binks and Bob Snape
University of Bolton

Introduction

This paper is based upon two Sport England funded research projects established in the summer of 2003 to evaluate the role of sport and physical activity in, respectively, community safety and community cohesion. Initially it was anticipated that the research would seek to identify sports development programmes designed to address issues of community safety and cohesion and to evaluate the impact of these on the attitudes and behaviour of their client groups and on the communities in which they were delivered. However, as the research progressed it became apparent that the contribution of sports development to the government's strategic aims in community safety and cohesion was diverse and fragmented with little if any overall co-ordination or support. Moreover, in some cases sports development officers working in the delivery phase of programmes had only a vague understanding of the social and political objectives of these programmes. As the complexity of the context within which community sports development officers were operating became clear, and as the challenges of deploying sports development to support government policy objectives became more well defined, the emphasis of the research moved away from the evaluation of practice, though not abandoning this altogether, towards an appraisal of the policy and implementation framework of contemporary community sports development.

The first section of this paper outlines the changing political context within which policy on community development is formulated and implemented and examines the implications of this for community sports development. The following sections provide a descriptive evaluation of the deployment of sports development in community safety and community cohesion initiatives and an evaluative assessment of the changing socio-political framework of community sports development.

The emerging political context of community sports development

A fundamental shift in the policy and planning framework of community sports development in recent years has been the change of emphasis from sports development in the community to community development through sport. The pace of this change has quickened since the general election of 1997 and the introduction by New Labour of a 'third way' approach to community development which, as noted by Popple and Redmond (2000), has utilised community development as a means of delivering a range of policy initiatives to address social exclusion in its economic, social and cultural manifestations. Within this approach it is common to find sport enthusiastically championed as a vehicle for the attainment of a range of social objectives as can be seen, for example, in Home Office website documentation on Active Communities, Positive Futures, Neighbourhood Renewal and Community Cohesion (Home Office, 2004).

A further tenet of the incoming Blair government was that of 'joined-up thinking' — a process through which strategic objectives would be addressed by a coordinated cross-departmental approach. The research thus provided an opportunity to assess the extent to which safety and cohesion initiatives emanating from the Home Office were supported by a joined-up, collaborative approach from other government departments and statutory bodies, particularly those concerned with sport. New Labour has also placed a special emphasis on developing and implementing policy initiatives through integrated local action (Newman, 2001), an approach which has led to a dominant pattern of community development work being undertaken though local partnerships of public, voluntary and private sector bodies, the governance of which is usually the responsibility of local authorities. Governance in this context requires a facility to effect a multi-agency approach to local issues through which trust and informality between partners — for example voluntary sports clubs, youth agencies and crime prevention bodies

— may be encouraged (Benyon and Edwards, 1999: pp. 148–150). However, as the effectiveness of multi-agency partnerships has been questioned (Bonney, 2004; Painter and Clarence, 2001: p. 1225; Reid, 1999; Wilson and Game, 2002: pp. 140–145), the research also sought to identify the impact of the partnership approach on the use of sport as a tool of community development.

Sport and community safety

The North West region of England currently has a wide variety of agencies delivering initiatives and programmes linked to community safety and antisocial behaviour. Numerous voluntary, charitable, local authority and national government agencies and organisations are woven within a pattern of initiative provision through local strategic partnerships. The scope and scale of provision of these has led to the development of a highly complex implementation framework, and while it was initially anticipated that a definitive picture of current provision within the North West could be achieved, it was soon accepted that this was impractical and the aim of the study was adapted. An indicative list of some of the relevant agencies and policy initiatives within the region was created and through an analytical review of these an attempt was made to identify good practice where it existed. The research also sought to explore staff perceptions of current issues linked to working practice. Key personnel in eight organisations, selected on a basis of accessibility and regional profile, were contacted and data collection was undertaken through semi-standardised interviews. These interviews focused on the role of the respective agency in the delivery of sports-related initiatives targeted at those whose behaviour was most likely to exercise negative impacts on safety issues within their communities. The complexity of the framework of this provision is illustrated in the following non-exhaustive list of relevant agencies operating in the North West:

- Ambassadors in Sport (Christian Foundation)
- Big Youth Project (Liverpool)
- Bolton Lads and Girls Club
- Connexions
- Crime Concern
- Crime and Disorder Reduction Partnerships
- Criminal Justice Intervention Programmes
- Crime Reduction Teams

- Community Safety Partnerships
- Fairbridge
- Local Authorities
- National Association for the Care and Resettlement of Offenders
- Neighbourhood Renewal Unit
- Police and Youth Encouragement Scheme (Merseyside)
- Positive Activities for Young People
- Positive Futures
- Prince's Trust
- Safer School Partnerships
- Youth Justice Boards (23 within the North West region)
- Youth Offending Teams
- Youth Inclusion Programmes
- Youth Inclusion and Support Panels
- Youth Charter for Sport, Culture and the Arts (Salford)

Common issues in community sports development and community safety

While most respondents were aware that community safety was primarily the responsibility of the Home Office, there was widespread scepticism concerning the roles of the Department for Culture, Media and Sport and of Sport England in supporting community safety initiatives. Indeed, several respondents indicated that they felt as if they were operating in a knowledge vacuum. There was a perception that provision was driven by funding, with initiatives being forced to operate in a reactive manner to short and medium term funding changes, thus leading to a patchwork pattern of delivery with a lack of coherence and a high level of confusion. Staff articulated feelings of insecurity, isolation and alienation, especially in situations in which there had been a history of interdepartmental rivalries between and within partnership organisations. Managers expressed concerns about the problems of retaining staff in situations in which short term funding regimes meant that little security of tenure could be given to those working in the delivery phase of programmes, while sports development workers described perceptions of unrealistic social objectives, duplication of effort and of being powerless to influence strategic planning. These difficulties were compounded through low staffing levels, a lack of professional advice and guidance and an emphasis in practice on reacting to short-term issues of operational management rather than to long-term strategic objectives.

A pattern of provision in which initiatives of a limited lifespan were serially replaced at the end of their funding period by new initiatives had been established as a norm in many communities. Consequently, continuity of engagement with client groups was a major issue for staff involved in delivery and fragmented engagement often led to difficulties in recruiting stakeholders and in eliciting the necessary commitment of goodwill from volunteers. Perhaps inevitably, experience of working in this environment led to a degree of cynicism concerning the feasibility of managing the complex partnerships through which many programmes operated. As a result of this, staff working in the delivery phase of programmes commonly adapted the stated aims of the programmes to fit perceptions of practicality, rather than re-designing programmes to meet complex and seemingly abstract objectives.

In addressing some of the problems identified above, several organisations were seeking to improve the delivery of initiatives through the development of systems of improved communication within local partnerships. The Joint Action Group established in Knowsley, Merseyside, for example, enabled individual agencies to coordinate resources, to adopt a strategic perspective on agreed targets and to develop common practice between and across partners. There was a widespread view that all levels of client activity should be tracked and several initiatives had developed computerised systems for achieving this end. There was also an emerging realisation that where success had been achieved, this often correlated to the employment of personnel from within the community in which an initiative was being delivered and to the resultant empathy with current community issues and perceptions. It was, however, noted that staff thus recruited developed transferable skills that enabled them to progress their careers elsewhere.

Sport and the Community Cohesion Pathfinders

The Community Cohesion Pathfinder programme was established in October 2002 and launched in April 2003 in response to the riots of the summer of 2001 in the post-industrial northern towns of Bradford, Oldham and Burnley. With the demise of their textile industries these towns had, like several others in Lancashire and Yorkshire, experienced prolonged economic decline since the Second World War and each had a large ethnic minority population of South Asian communities. The majority of the participants in the riots were males aged between 17 and 26, drawn from both white and Asian ethnic minority groups. The *Cantle Report* (Home Office, 2001), commissioned by the government to investigate the causes of the disturbances, noted that the towns in which the riots had occurred comprised ethnic communities which were markedly separated in language, culture, faith and education and described a pattern of 'parallel lives' in which members of differing ethnic communities led separate existences and rarely came into social contact with members of other communities. In April 2002 the Home Office established the Community Cohesion Unit and in January 2003 the first phase of the Community Cohesion Pathfinder programme was introduced in 14 Pathfinder areas which covered between them 23 local authority areas. The Pathfinder programme adopted the interpretation of a cohesive community published in the Local Government Association's *Guidance* (2002) which described a cohesive community as one in which

- there was a common vision and a sense of belonging for all communities;
- the diversity of people's different backgrounds and circumstances was appreciated and positively valued;
- those from different backgrounds had similar life opportunities;
- strong and positive relationships were being developed between people from different backgrounds within neighbourhoods.

The objective of the Community Cohesion Pathfinders was thus not only to promote cultural diversity and equality of opportunity but to instigate interaction and promote social and cultural relationships between differing communities. In terms of sport this implied not simply the enhancement of access to sport as prescribed in *Achieving racial equality: a standard for sport* (Commission for Racial Equality, 2001) but challenging patterns of 'parallel lives' in sport by bringing together traditionally separated communities in integrated sporting activity and by using sport to develop relationships between individuals and communities.

The research project focused on the three Pathfinders established in the north west of England in Bury, Rochdale and East Lancashire, the latter being a regional Pathfinder embracing Accrington, Burnley, Nelson, Colne and the Rossendale Valley. It was conducted through semi-structured interviews with personnel in both planning and operational capacities in the public and voluntary sectors over an eleven month period from October 2003 to August 2004. All three Pathfinders had used sports development to support their aims because of sport's popular appeal across differing ethnic groups and because, as one respondent stated, it offered a relatively neutral cultural territory in which to engage young and in many cases disaffected people in a shared activity. However, there were methodological variations in the ways in which sport was deployed.

A guiding principle of the Community Cohesion Pathfinder programme was that Pathfinders should determine their own priorities in the light of local circumstances and issues. Although in practice sport was used in each Pathfinder, the extent to which it featured at the strategic planning stage, as reflected in published aims and objectives, varied. In one Pathfinder, for example, in which a previous Director of Leisure Services was a member of the local Pathfinder Steering Group, there was a specific commitment to implement a wide range of sports projects to promote cohesion while in others sport received no such specific reference.

In each area, the Pathfinder gave an impetus, and in some cases direct funding, to the development of sporting activities designed to facilitate community integration. Bury Metropolitan Borough Council, for example, used part of its Pathfinder allocation to fund the appointment of a Football Development Officer (Inclusion) with a brief to co-ordinate football development across the borough with an emphasis on the integration of the white and Asian communities and of asylum seekers in football activity. In Burnley a project was established in conjunction with the Community Safety programme to co-ordinate a series of curriculum enrichment activities to promote themes of anti-racism and cultural respect in all schools in the borough which was to be followed by a mini-Olympics at Turf Moor, the ground of Burnley Football Club, to which children and their families would be invited. Rochdale Leisure Services established Rochdale Partners through Sport which aimed to involve young people aged 11–19 years and to reduce racial tensions between communities. Rochdale also provided financial support, through its Pathfinder funding, to initiate Sports United, a project managed through the Rochdale Federation of Tenants' and Residents' Associations which sought to use football and other sports as a means of engaging Asian and white young people in integrated sport activity and in programmed workshops on cultural diversity, racism and community safety.

The Community Cohesion Pathfinders thus stimulated interest in the potential role of sport in promoting community cohesion and provided the impetus for a number of imaginative programmes of activity. However, the research also revealed some challenges and difficulties. The complexity of partnership-based funding streams through which money was drawn from a variety of sources may have been efficacious in certain instances but at least one major sport development project was curtailed at mid-point because the advice it had been given on accessing a community fund had been "very woolly and changed several times" and as a result several hundred thousand pounds of funding had been withdrawn from the project. Elsewhere a voluntary community association had successfully launched five-a-side football programmes with integrated participation by white and Asian youths. However this could not be further developed, not so much because funding was unavailable but because the organisation, which did not have staff management expertise in sport or leisure management, did not know where to seek help or guidance. Other occurrences were found in which personnel with a management brief to promote cohesion yet lacking a professional background in the leisure sector wished to initiate sport activity but were frustrated by difficulties in bidding for funding. In some cases this frustration gave vent to expressions of disappointment that statutory agencies with a responsibility to support and fund community sport did not appear to be actively supporting the Cohesion Pathfinders. Although anecdotal, this evidence is supported both by the Home Office itself, which through its own mid-point evaluation of the Pathfinder programmes highlighted a strong feeling that "central government could do more to deliver a joined-up approach to community cohesion" (Home Office, 2003). One year later, the lack of integration on community cohesion at Cabinet level was acknowledged by the Home Office's Community Cohesion Panel in its statement that:

> Whilst the Home Office has been pursuing a cross departmental agenda, there is not yet the ownership within other departments and most have failed to integrate community cohesion and equality. We have learnt that a Government policy led by one Department does not always have the ownership of others and, indeed, may be resisted by them as it is seen as 'just a Home Office issue'. We believe that all Government Departments should produce and publish action plans on community cohesion and would particularly welcome strong contributions from the Office of the Deputy Prime Minister, Department of Culture, Media and Sport [sic] and Department for Education and Skills, where there is significant potential for cross-cultural contact to be developed. (Community Cohesion Unit, 2004: p. 18)

The temporary nature of the Community Cohesion Pathfinders was a further area of concern to some of those involved, either because of a cynicism that this was, in the words of one respondent, "just another funding stream" which would not be extended or because their two and a half years time span was not considered sufficiently long to make more than small progress towards such a complex objective.

The changing socio-political framework of community sports development

The role of sport as an agent in interventionist strategies in the areas of community safety and community cohesion was diverse in form and complex in structure, and is illustrative of the context of sport in terms of New Labour's third way approach to community development. Both initiatives emanated from the Home Office, and both therefore had social and not sport objectives. The extent to which sport development programmes were able to obtain funding to support community safety or cohesion objectives thus depended on a clear articulation of social or community benefits and in some areas this led to the imaginative and potentially useful action described above. In other areas there was a lack of clarity of understanding of the objectives of the initiatives among some of those involved in sports development and concomitant difficulties in formulating targets for sports programmes that fully reflected those of the respective initiative. This occurred in community cohesion where, for example, some of the proposed sporting activities were primarily concerned with enhancing equality of access to sport for ethnic minorities as an end in itself rather than as an initial step to promoting ethnically integrated participation. It is, however, too easy to be critical of this given the magnitude of the aims of the Cohesion Pathfinders and at an early stage of the programme it became evident that political and community leaders commonly experienced difficulties in distinguishing community cohesion from other related agendas such as race relations (Home Office, 2003). This lack of understanding may also be attributable to the contested nature of community cohesion; the Home Office's interpretation (Community Cohesion Unit, 2002) is, for example, much more simplistic than that developed through academic models in its exclusion of potential causes of lack of cohesion (Kearns and Forrest, 2000; Forrest and Kearns, 2001), particularly that of economic deprivation. Elsewhere, notably in community safety initiatives, there was a tendency to express targets in terms of numbers engaged or of social control rather than any form of dynamic change within communities, reflecting previous findings of trends in the evaluation of sports development identified by Long and Sanderson (2001: pp. 201–202).

The research also provided insights to the changing political and policy context of community sport development. Under New Labour policy making has been informed by the concept of social inclusion, a retreat from universal welfarism and the targeting of resources at the socially excluded and thus an emphasis on sport for specified groups rather than sport for all. This has been accompanied by a desire to establish a sustainable, coherent and co-ordinated approach to community regeneration. Given the apparent impracticability and inefficiency of overarching plans and centralised approaches to the needs of specific communities and the failure of historical models of service delivery, New Labour's third way has led to a model of community sports development which is grounded in a local strategic partnership approach to community regeneration. In theory this should facilitate joined-up planning and operational delivery, a redirection of public funding towards areas of greater need and an integrated multi-agency plan for specific localities. In practice, the perception at community level amongst sport development workers is that funding, and to a certain extent planning, has not followed this approach.

Many of the respondents engaged in community sport development reported feelings of isolation and of being poorly informed on the nature and origins of the social objectives towards which they were working. Together with the predominant pattern of short-term contracts and the unpredictability of future funding this contributed a sense of personal insecurity and pessimism concerning the sustainability of many programmes. Of particular note was the impact of the partnership approach on the role of sports development, and it is useful here to consider not only the normative concept of partnership in this context as an integration of local public, voluntary and private sector bodies but also the implied sense of partnership at government level in terms of New Labour's pursuit of joined-up thinking. As indicated above, this was perceived by some community development managers to be lacking, a perception clearly vindicated through the above mentioned Home Office comments concerning the reluctance of the Department for Culture, Media and Sport to support actively its policy initiatives.

A final note concerns the ontological status of community sports development and the implications of this for the training and education of those who work within it. While in the past community development has relied upon professional leisure managers to initiate and deliver community sports development, the Cohesion Pathfinders exhibited evidence of a shift from dependence on single function professionals to managerial professionals and from an historically central role of local authority leisure service departments to one in which the strategic deployment of sport, even at a local level, was becoming the domain of policy units within strategic partnerships (see Ravenscroft, 1998).

The changes outlined above point to a postmodern scenario cf community sports development and are illustrated in Table1.

Table1:   *The changing socio-political context of community sports development.*

Historic context of community sports development		New socio-political context of community sports development	
Universal welfarism	*Sport for All*	Targeted public provision	*Social inclusion*
Grand Plan	*Social Democratic / Liberal ideologies*	Big Idea	*Third Way*
Centralisation	*Sports Council, Local Authority Leisure Services*	Decentralisation	*Local Strategic Partnerships, Unelected bodies*
Operational Management	*Focus on delivery*	Strategic Management	*Focus on managerialism and evaluation*
Simple objectives	*Quantitative*	Complex objectives	*Quantitative and Qualitative*
Single Task	*Sport as social control, e.g. for youth, unemployed or increased participation*	Multiple Task	*Sport as a tool of complex social change*
Sustained and secure funding	*Direct and indirect state / local authority funding*	Competitive and insecure funding	*Bidding culture and uncertainty*
Permanence	*Long term planning and budgetary continuity*	Ephemerality	*Projects, Pathfinders, short term initiatives and constant change*
Autonomy	*Use of sport the domain of sport professionals*	Partnership	*Use of sport the domain of social policy professionals*
Permanent employment	*Traditional public sector employment, local government leisure officers*	Temporary contracts	*Community Sport Development workers, project staff*

After Harvey, D. (1990) *The condition of postmodernity* : pp. 340–341.

Moving to a postmodern framework of community sports development

The pattern of the management and operation of sport development initiatives to support community safety and cohesion in the north west region reveals an emerging paradox. At a time when the government is attempting to develop a coordinated multi-agency approach to addressing social issues, the reality for those who are involved in the delivery of community sports development initiatives is one of fragmentation, isolation and ambiguity. Where organisations and initiatives are cooperating, this is often through necessity rather than choice. The high levels of ambiguity experienced by those delivering programmes are leading to high levels of anxiety and, in turn, feelings of insecurity. Where positive joined- up outcomes are being achieved through a collaborative joined –up approach they are underpinned by highly contextualised inter and/or intra organisation / initiative communication structures. Where positive outcomes are being achieved in isolation, however, community sports development personnel often believe that they are succeeding in spite of the perceived levels and types of available support. At a national level the government faces the challenge of balancing policy coherence and control with community need and of ensuring that all departments, and notably in the current context the Department for Culture, Media and Sport, support central policy initiatives. This has implications for government at regional level which must recognise the complexity of the situation described above and develop a relevant and coherent strategy for the removal of perceptions of ambiguity and insecurity at all levels of programme intervention.

References

Benyon, J. and Edwards, A. (1999) 'Community governance of crime control', in G. Stoker (ed) *The new management of British local governance.* Basingstoke: Macmillan. pp. 145–167.

Bonney, N. (2004) 'Local democracy renewed?', *Political Quarterly* Vol. 75, No.1: pp. 43–51.

Commission for Racial Equality (2001) *Achieving racial equality: A standard for sport.* London, CRE.

Community Cohesion Unit (2002) *Guidance on community cohesion.* London: Home Office.

Community Cohesion Unit (2004) *The end of parallel lives? The report of the Community Cohesion Panel.* London: Home Office.

Forrest, R. and Kearns, A. (2001) 'Social cohesion, social capital and the neighbourhood,' *Urban Studies* Vol. 38, No.12: pp. 2125–2143.

Harvey, D. (1990) *The condition of postmodernity: An enquiry into the origins of cultural change.* Oxford: Blackwell.

Home Office (2001) *Community Cohesion: a report of the Independent Review Team chaired by Ted Cantle.* London, Home Office.

Home Office (2003) *Community Cohesion Pathfinder Programme: The first six months.* London: Home Office.

Home Office (2004) www.homeoffice.gov.uk 19th August.

Kearns, A. and Forrest, R., (2000), 'Social cohesion and multi-level urban governance', *Urban Studies* Vol. 37, Nos. 5–6: pp. 995–1017.

Local Government Association (2002) *Draft guidance on community cohesion.* London: LGA.

Long, J. and Sanderson, I. (2001) 'The social benefits of sport. Where's the proof?' in C. Gratton and I. Henry (eds) *Sport in the city: the role of sport in economic and social regeneration.* London: Routledge, pp. 187–203.

Newman, J. (2001) *Modernising governance: New Labour, policy and society.* London: Sage.

Painter, C. and Clarence, E. (2001) 'UK Local Action Zones and changing urban governance', *Urban Studies* Vol. 38, No. 8: pp. 1215–1232.

Popple, K. and Redmond, M. (2000) 'Community development and the voluntary sector in the new millennium: The implications of the Third Way', *Community Development Journal* Vol. 35, No. 4: pp. 391–400.

Ravenscroft, N. (1998) 'The changing regulation of public sector leisure provision', *Leisure Studies* Vol. 17, No. 2: pp: 138–154.

Reid, B. (1999) 'Reframing the delivery of local housing services: networks and the new competition', in G. Stoker (ed) *The new management of British local governance.* Basingstoke: Macmillan, pp. 128–144.

Wilson, D. and Game, C. (2002) *Local government in the United Kingdom.* Basingstoke: Palgrave.

II

DIFFERENCE, YOUNG PEOPLE
AND PARTICIPATION

DOING SPORT, DOING INCLUSION: AN ANALYSIS OF PROVIDER AND PARTICIPANT PERCEPTIONS OF TARGETED SPORT PROVISION FOR YOUNG MUSLIMS

James Lowrey and Tess Kay
Institute of Youth Sport, Loughborough University

Introduction

This paper investigates whether sports provision targeted at young people from local minority ethnic communities can contribute to 'inclusion'. Its focus is a current development project providing a combined programme of sport and education activities, designed to encourage young people to progress to higher levels of education beyond the age of compulsory schooling. The project is based in a town in the Midlands (referred to as 'town' throughout this paper) where the local population of approximately 57,000 is predominantly white but includes a number of minority ethnic communities. The project reflects the Labour government's education agenda, within which the government has paid particular attention to those aged 16–18 years who are outside of education, of whom many are also not employed. The age of 16 has been seen as a critical point in young people's life trajectories, when young people move out of compulsory education and start what might be a more unstructured phase of life. The early phases of this are periods during which problems can often begin which are ultimately costly to the individual and to society generally. This paper considers whether sport can be an appropriate basis for interventions to address this situation.

The policy context: sport and social inclusion

Sport is one of a number of policy tools that has been brought to bear on issues of social inclusion surrounding young people. In 1999 the Policy Action Team 10 report for the Social Exclusion unit (Department for Culture, Media and

Sport (DCMS), 1999) suggested that sport and the arts could make a substantial contribution to all four areas of social exclusion policy — education, employment, crime prevention and health. Academics have been more sceptical, acknowledging the theoretical benefits of sport but emphasising the lack of evidence that such benefits are actually achieved (e.g. Coalter *et al.*, 2000; Collins *et al.*, 1999; Long *et al.*, 2002). Notwithstanding this, there has been a marked increase in sports-based provision addressing social exclusion issues.

The research reported here examines the impact of sport as a mechanism for engaging young people from minority ethnic groups and encouraging them to progress to further and/or higher education. This remit means that the project on which the study is based addressed a number of priority themes within social inclusion policy. Firstly, its target group involved both young people, a primary focus for inclusion policy, and members of minority ethnic groups, identified as the social group most exposed to social exclusion. Secondly, it was designed to contribute specifically to education policy, seen as critical in the long-term strategy to develop a more inclusive society.

The importance attached to addressing young people's progression to education was evident early in the lifetime of the first Blair government. In 1999 the Social Exclusion Unit produced *Bridging the Gap* (Social Exclusion Unit, 1999), a report that suggested that there was no real structure for those who did not move on to further/higher education after completing compulsory education. Those that fall into this group were said to be disproportionately from backgrounds where they would experience social exclusion, while the lack of the direction for this age group heightened their likelihood of experiencing further exclusion later in life. To deal with the young people who were not in post compulsory education or employment the government established a new youth support service, seeing this as a long term plan that "would need to be implemented progressively, and would take some time to achieve results" (Social Exclusion Unit, 1999: p. 13). The main aim of the new service was to ensure "young people stay in education, training, or work with a strong education/training component until they are at least 18" (Social Exclusion Unit, 1999: p. 9). A key policy target of the government to ensure increased educational participation, was that of "graduation". "Graduation would be a challenging but achievable goal requiring as a minimum the level 2 standard of achievement in formal qualifications" (Social Exclusion Unit: 1999: p. 11). Financial support (Education Maintenance Allowances) was increased with the aim of seeing whether supporting young people in full-time education with extra finances increased participation levels. From September 2004 Education Maintenance Allowances were made available throughout England. A new personal support service was also developed to "steer young people" between the ages of 13 and 19 through education. Within this service priority would be given to those who are identified as being at risk of "underachievement and disaffection".

With the government's emphasis on improving opportunities for young people aged 16–18, further and higher education institutions have adopted a much greater focus on widening participation than they have done in the past. The Higher Education Funding Council for England (HEFCE) suggested that "participation in higher education will equip people to operate productively within the global knowledge economy. It also offers social benefits, including better health, lower crime and a more tolerant and inclusive society" (HEFCE website: 2004). The widening of opportunities for those who are under-represented within FE and HE is a key aim of the current government. The Secretary of State in *The Future of Higher Education (2003)* stated that "we must make certain that the opportunities that higher education brings are available to all those who have the potential to benefit from them, regardless of their background" (The Future of Higher Education, Page 67, 2003). To date, however, achievements appear to have been limited: in 2003 the number of young people aged 16–18 in full-time education was 56.5%, only a slight increase from 55.7% in 2001. (Department for Education and Skills (DfES), June 2004). These levels compare poorly with other countries: in 2003 the United Kingdom was ranked 27th out of 30 developed nations for participation of 17-year-olds in learning (DfES, 2004).

Many of those that are seen to be underachieving within education are from minority ethnic groups, in particular young people from Black and Asian (but not Indian) communities:

> Young people of Pakistani and Bangladeshi origin are particularly likely to experience lengthy spells of non-participation, with one in six experiencing spells of four or more months in the 22 months following the end of compulsory education. (Social Exclusion Unit, 1999: p. 22)

Non-participation among minority ethnic groups is often linked to their experience of pre-16 education and the "lack of understanding" and "support" from teachers, as well as "ignorant comments based on stereotyping about career goals, family and community cultures" (Social Exclusion Unit, 1999: p. 40). The *Bridging the Gap* report highlighted how young people from minority ethnic communities face 'additional and particular barriers' when trying to find employment. Two out of five 16 year olds from minority ethnic groups in 1997 not in full-time education were out of work, compared to one in five of their white counterparts. There is little improvement with age: 13% of men under 35 from ethnic minorities have spent more than one third of their lives since 16 unemployed, compared to 7% for young white men (Social Exclusion Unit, 1999).

The research within this paper focuses upon two widening participation initiatives that were operating in a Midlands University between 2001–2004. The focus of the project was sport and its usefulness as a vehicle for encouraging young people from Black and minority ethnic (BME) communities to enter further and higher education.

Methodology

The aims of this research were two-fold: first to evaluate the *concept* of using sport as a mechanism for promoting inclusion among minority ethnic groups; and, second, to evaluate the *actual response* to a programme of provision based on the principles identified in the first phase.

The first phase of the research was undertaken as part of an evaluation of the Higher Education Participation Through Sport (HEPTS) project, a pilot initiative funded by the HEFCE. The research into this project was designed to increase understanding of the extent to which sport could be used to engage young people from BME communities and encourage them to progress to Further/Higher Education (FE/HE) (Kay and Lowrey, 2003). As part of the evaluation the research aimed to highlight the issues that were of importance to the young people within sport and education. The two aims of this phase of the research were:

- to identify barriers, actual and perceptual, that prevent BME young people from participating in sport and education;
- to develop an understanding of the usefulness of sport as a vehicle for encouraging BME young people to enter FE/HE.

Interviews (10) were conducted with professionals (Local authority workers, community centre managers, racial equality staff, FE/HE employees, sport development workers) and voluntary workers (mentors, youth group leaders, community workers) experienced in working with young people from BME communities. All the interviews were semi-structured, tape recorded, and transcribed. The data collected is reported in the first results section of this paper.

The HEPTS pilot project was the precursor to a more substantial sport-education programme, the Widening Access Through Sport (WATS) project. WATS, which was funded by the European Social Fund to run for 2 years (2003–04), built on the principles identified through HEPTS, offering activities that were attended by small groups of young people over an extended period. The second phase of the research focused on the experiences of these participants and their perspectives on the value and relevance of WATS to their situation.

In this paper, particular attention is paid to young people aged 14–19 from the Bangladeshi community in the town in which the university was located. Four focus groups were undertaken with participants (n=20) from the WATS project, to identify whether the factors important to them within sport and education reflected the issues identified as being important by the professional and voluntary workers. Semi-structured in-depth interviews were also undertaken with the two WATS Project Workers in 'Town' to gain their insights into the impact of the project on the participants. All focus groups and interviews were tape-recorded, transcribed, and the data was analysed thematically.

Results 1: the concept of provision

The research conducted into the HEPTS project collected data from a wide range of professional and voluntary workers. The workers identified a number of interwoven reasons for low participation levels among BME young people within sport, and several issues that needed to be addressed if sports-based projects were to be attractive to these groups.

The 'community insider'

The first major factor identified within the research was the importance of having an 'insider' when working with BME communities, a person from the targeted community who worked on behalf of the project with the targeted population. Through interviews with professionals this was identified as the key factor behind getting youngsters from BME communities involved in sport. If a recognised member of the target community believed in the value of the project, they would find it relatively easy to 'sell' the project to young people. In contrast, anyone regarded as an outsider could be treated with hostility and suspicion. The insider on the other hand would be well placed to deal with the young people, as s/he would understand the issues that were of importance:

> "It's more conducive to have Asian officers who understand the big picture and can go and sell to another Asian group, than a white person coming in ... people engage more with people they feel safer around and that is usually their own culture." [*Sports Service Manager*]

Ideally the "insider" would be well known within the community and would have, or be able to gain, the respect and trust of the younger and older generations. Credibility with the older generation was important for facilitating access to the young people. If the young people see one of the older members of their community supporting a sports programme then they themselves might see the project as being worthwhile. This can also spread onto other young people and parents within the community, a snowball effect can occur when word reaches more and more members of the community about the targeted sports provision:

> "Every time whenever the parent asks where are you going they would reply for example I am going to Town University, so it is always thrown up, and the more use they make of that terminology and they associate it with the university, the more of a relationship they can build." [*Voluntary Community Worker*]

The member(s) of the community employed could also act as role model figures for the young people. The young people would see the community worker organising sports events, and some might then be encouraged to undertake a similar role when they are older. Having role models that the young people can look up to was said to be one technique that could contribute towards increasing participation levels. It was crucial that the young people could see somebody of a similar background to themselves in these roles.

> "The key focus ... needs to be on the leaders because the leaders are the best placed people when they come from that local community and what we need to do is get other leaders from the ethnic groups actually leading the sessions, leading those kind of sessions because they know what the issues are ... they are the obvious role model." [*Sport Through Education Project Officer*]

Family influence

The second main theme identified through the data collected was the importance of the family. The role that the family plays in influencing their child's participation within sport was stated as an issue that had to be considered for a number of reasons. Family influence is especially significant among Asian communities, in which "family" is a particularly central institution.

The first issue raised was that the limited value attached to sport within some families might prevent the young people from taking part. Several of the HEPTS interviewees felt that in some communities, sport is seen as unproductive. Education and family responsibilities are seen as more constructive ways for young people to spend their time. In relation to the HEPTS project, it was noted that in many Bangladeshi households within Town, sons in particular provided financial support to the family. This had implications not only for current participation in sport, but also for attitudes towards future education and employment prospects:

> "In the Bangladeshi community ... a lot of the families make their money through shops and restaurants and takeaways ... locally their kids are a real resource for them ... family is your strength, if their family leaves and goes to university they will miss them massively, not just love wise, financially they will miss them because those kids bring in income by working in the restaurants ... so you have got a very small close-knit community and they are raising their kids to just take over their businesses." [*Education Through Sport Project Officer*]

Additional factors could apply among the Muslim community, affecting the participation of daughters. Parents of Muslim young women might have concerns that the facilities for the sports sessions would not be suitable. Some of the professional workers noted that the fear of sports sessions not being female-only, might prevent some youngsters participating. Prayer times were another concern mentioned. The fear that prayers might not be incorporated into the sports sessions would be a barrier that could prevent parents agreeing to their son/daughter attending a session. It was noted however that if the "insider" had the trust of the local community and ensured the appropriate arrangements were in place, they would be able to reassure parents and gain their support, therefore ensuring the young people could participate. The significance of the relationship between development workers and parents was emphasised by a local voluntary worker:

> "Our parents speak very little English so they themselves lack in confidence, we trust they send their kids to us and we look after them." [*Community Worker*]

This language barrier was a concern that many professional workers noted as another reason behind parents preventing their children taking part in sports events. Many parents within the Bangladeshi community in Town had limited competence in English and were reluctant to let their child attend activities they did not feel fully informed about. To overcome this, literature needed to be written in appropriate languages. Not only would this help older members of the community understand what provisions are being organised but it would also show a willingness on the part of the organisers to meet the needs of the targeted population. Language can be a significant barrier to participation:

> "If somebody wants to book some facility and speaks Hindu or Gujerati now how does that person engage with a white person that doesn't speak that language? And so already you have got this barrier which people can't get over and so they don't go." [*Sports Service Manager*]

Ideally the "community insider" would be able to overcome this problem through communicating in a language that the targeted community felt confident using.

The "comfort" factor

Feeling welcome and comfortable was a point mentioned by nearly all of the voluntary and professional workers. If the young person did not feel welcome within the setting then there would be little hope of encouraging them to regularly participate in sports. As well as "feeling welcome", many professionals and voluntary workers said that the young person would need to feel comfortable. They distinguished between a young person being welcomed to a new setting, and whether they actually felt comfortable once they were within it. Bringing a group of young Muslims to a university campus for example could be a daunting experience for the youngsters and therefore efforts would have to be made by the institution to ensure the needs of the group were met. On the one hand, this could be achieved by taking sports provision to the young people within a familiar setting preferably in their own locality; this familiarity would ensure that the comfort factor would not be an issue. If, however, sport was being used to promote further and higher education, it could be valuable to locate activities in the relevant university or college, to help build familiarity with the institution. Participating and becoming comfortable in the university or college setting could raise the awareness of the young people about what an FE/HE institution would be like and encourage them to investigate the educational opportunities that exist.

> "If the university … if they offered incentives to the youngsters to use the university facilities they would become familiar with the university then it could promote its activities and its courses to the youngsters very easily without them running away." (*Community Worker*).

Linked with this, a recurring issue within the research was that of "addressing needs". This was seen as being crucial to the success of any sports programmes. One of the biggest barriers for young Muslim women participating in sport is often the lack of suitable facilities. Facilities used would have to have female-only access, the sports programmes put together would have to be run by female instructors, and usual codes of dress might have to be changed. Throughout the research it was emphasised that these and other religious and cultural needs were important factors to consider. Prayer times for example would have to be incorporated into any activities:

> "You have to cater for their needs and you can only do that by going to the actual community leaders and talk about what University are prepared to do … but you can't make that person who's going for prayer feel ostracised because he needs to pray, it needs to be a natural format or a natural kind of break to make somebody feel comfortable." [*Sports Service Manager*]

Many professional workers also highlighted perceptual barriers. Interviewees commented on the fact that young people particularly from the Bangladeshi community wouldn't see the university as being for them. Views that "people like us don't go there" and "nobody there will be dressed like us" were mentioned by voluntary workers as reasons for young people from the Bangladeshi community being reluctant to attend organised sport events. According to one community worker the university would generally be seen as "off limits" for the young people.

Results 2: the reality of provision

Through funding received from the European Social Fund the WATS project was established at Town University. The project aimed to work with 60–80 young people from BME communities within Leicestershire, aged between 14 and 19, between January 2003 and December 2004. The results reported in this section of the paper relate to two groups of Muslim participants from the local community in Town.

Town has a population of approximately 57,000 and is located in the East Midlands of England, UK. Town is split into ten wards, each having a population between 5,000–7,000. The Bangladeshi community, which totals 1221, is largely concentrated in two wards, within which it accounts for 12% and 9% of the total ward population respectively. Many Bangladeshi workers have a poor command of English and have been employed in the past, in companies where Bengali was spoken on a day-to-day basis. The Bangladeshi community has been identified as having skills needs, low levels of qualifications and low economic activity rates linked to a poor command of English (Borough Economic Profile, 2001).

The WATS project aimed to "improve access to post-compulsory education for young people from BME communities in Leicestershire, through the innovative use of sport-education activity programmes as pathways to FE and HE opportunities". The idea underlying this was that sport could be used to engage with the young people; once "engaged" the project would then then try to raise their awareness of the further and higher education opportunities available to them. These could be sport-related (e.g. courses leading to qualifications in sports science, leisure management etc) although this was not the primary goal of the project.

In Town, two development workers were appointed to work with young women and young men from the local Muslim community. Drawing on the experience of the HEPTS project, and guided by the expertise of the development workers appointed to the project, WATS established a range of integrated sport and education programmes. Various sports were undertaken by the young people, alongside an education syllabus based on the Connexions' 'Getting Connected' syllabus. The Connexions syllabus is centred on personal development, with increasing self confidence and self-esteem being key components of most units. The female group based in Town also undertook a Community Coaching Qualification to become qualified Level One netball coaches.

All the male sport and education sessions were undertaken at the university campus. As the young women were unable to participate in activities during the evenings or weekends due to family commitments, they undertook their education sessions at school during their lunch breaks and then came to the university campus during school/college holidays to undertake intensive sport, and further educational, activities.

Response to the targeted provision: the role of the Community Insiders

On the basis of the HEPTS project findings, WATS aimed to employ project workers who came from within the target communities who would have continuous contact with the young people and would see the youngsters outside the project activity sessions. The workers would deliver the core sport and education sessions themselves but could call on "expert" sessional staff, e.g. sports instructors or coaches, when required.

The two project workers employed by WATS were members of Town's Bangladeshi community. Prior to the activity sessions beginning, discussions took place between the project management and the project workers about the appropriate content and delivery of the activities programmes. In turn the project workers consulted within the Bangladeshi community to identify what activities might be attractive to young men and women, allowing them to develop sport and education programmes which were based on what the young people wanted to do.

To analyse the impact and the success of the targeted sports provision interviews were conducted with the two project workers and focus groups were undertaken with all participants (N =20) on the Town projects. Many of the issues identified by the professional and voluntary workers in the background research were of importance to the young people on the WATS programmes. Firstly, the community insider was central to any work undertaken with the young Muslims. The participants frequently expressed the importance of having somebody who was similar to themselves, who could show them around the university and who would understand the issues that were of importance to them. This led to them feeling comfortable and relaxed within an environment which almost all had never entered before.

The project leaders were known to many of the young people prior to their participation on the WATS project; they had both worked in a voluntary capacity with the young people for a number of years. This automatically ensured a good relationship could be built, something that "outsiders" would not immediately have been able to develop. With the project workers also being from the same community as the targeted youth they acted as role models for the participants. When one female participant was asked by the group leader what she wanted to do after her compulsory education finished, she commented:

> "You know what you do ... I want to do that ... you know what like you are doing is good, I want to help. Give everybody the opportunity to get together and play sports, and especially cos' it's just girls because we don't get that at all, so I would like to do that." [*Female Participant*]

Being known to the young people and also to the community generally, meant that parental consent could be gained without too many problems:

> "Anything from outsiders, any project or initiative, they [the parents] are usually very cynical about it ... why does this person want to do this, what is his motive ... so there is a lot of cynicism, a negative feeling, whereas if it is me coming in then it gets rid of that feeling." [*WATS Male Project Worker*]

Combining education with sport contributed to the fact that many parents viewed the activities as good ways for their children to spend their time. Again, much of this seemed to reflect the credibility of the project workers:

> "I have had conversations with their parents and [initially] they actually do think that this is a waste of time ... only after having a dialogue with them and saying the aim of the project is not just to let them do sports and nothing else but use sports to try and get them onto higher education then they are more accepting." [*WATS Male Project Worker*]

Response to the targeted provision: the environment and comfort factor

Almost all the young people on the WATS projects in Town commented that without WATS they wouldn't be involved in many sports. The males commented that they might play football or basketball in the park but there wouldn't be the opportunities to participate in formal structured sports sessions. The young women suggested that they wouldn't be involved in any sports, and would instead spend their free time within the home watching TV or occasionally going into the town centre.

For the young Muslim women it was clear that the female-only sport sessions were crucial not only for their participation but also for their enjoyment. The local leisure centre was noted as a place where they could take part in sport but rarely would they feel comfortable and other people there would often stop and stare wondering why they were dressed they way they were:

> "It's like the leisure centre if you go everybody is dressed in a different way to you and they are staring at you instead of doing what they are meant to be doing." [*Female Participant*]

Sports within schools were also seen as problematic for the young girls:

> "It is different because the sports that we do at school there are guys as well and the sports we done here were just girls and that made you feel more relaxed and you could do whatever you wanted." [*Female Participant*]

The situation within their own group on the WATS project was very different. One girl expressed the feeling that she felt she was fully understood in a way in which she was not in other circumstances:

> "I get the impression when I say something that you [the group] understand what I am saying, I would say I don't know … my dad said no, I wouldn't have to sit down and say ' because of this, this and this, and explain myself. I feel that when I say something you get it and say yeah right." [*Female Participant*]

Lack of knowledge about what is actually available to them was one barrier clearly affecting the young Muslims' participation within sport. Many of the youngsters pass the university on their way to school but before the WATS project they didn't see the university as "being for them":

> "I never even knew they had all these facilities and nothing has ever been organised for us like this before." [*Male Participant*]

Another young person added:

> "I thought it specialised in sports … and they welcomed anyone who would do sports but I had my doubts about what will they think about a bunch of girls coming in, you know, doing sports as a laugh

but when I took part my opinions changed so with the university everything was great." [*Female Participant*]

The participants felt they would now feel comfortable coming back to the campus even if it was not part of the WATS project; however, although both males and females said they would be prepared to come back to the university in pairs, they would still prefer it if they were in a group again. From this it is clear that some steps forward have been made but members of the local Bangladeshi community would feel more comfortable coming to the campus with other members of their own community. Feeling comfortable was crucial to participants' enjoyment of the WATS programmes.

Response to the targeted provision: the wider community effect

Many of the youngsters on the WATS project mentioned that they had told friends and families about what they have been involved in. This "word of mouth" appeared to have strengthened the relationship between the university and the local Bangladeshi community. Some of the events organised as part of the WATS project have been opened up to larger numbers of youngsters:

> "The benefits of that is that more of the wider community have access to that facility, more of the wider community benefit from such sports taking place and when they are on the university ground ... they feel more comfortable so do they come as well ... and if things like this take place on a regular basis they feel a natural attachment ... hence Town University becomes our base in any activity. So automatically an attachment is built there." [*WATS Male Project Worker*]

Sports tournaments were used as events that larger numbers of young people could attend, during which they could gain an insight into the type of activities undertaken on the WATS project. The following conversation came from a group discussion from the female WATS group:

[1] "I go on about it all the time, they're like 'ok shut up!'"

[2] "They don't think we would be able to do something like that [karate]."

[1] "Especially cos' of the way we dress, they wouldn't think we could."

[2] "They are careful what they say to us now!."

The male project worker noted how one group of young males had come to the campus and organised their own football session. Not all of those involved in the session were from the WATS project but because word had spread within the community about the opportunities to participate in sport at the local university, the youngsters took it on board to organise their own activity. The positive experiences of the young Muslim men have obviously impacted upon other youngsters within the community. Not only did this serve to reinforce the relationship that has developed between the university and the local Bangladeshi community, but it has also helped promote WATS itself to future participants.

Analysis of targeted provision: the benefits for the participants

Alongside the sport, WATS participants undertook educational classes. The classes were kept informal and mainly focussed on personal development. The idea behind the education was to increase the confidence of the young people and encourage them to think about possible routes that they could take in further and higher education. Simply bringing the young people to a university campus at weekends and during school holidays raised their awareness of what the university was like.The response was very positive:

> "We are having fun, we are learning more about one another and higher education kind of life ... the atmosphere ... and we are developing our fitness, that's not just physically that is mentally as well." [*Female Participant*]

Raising awareness of university life was one of the primary objectives of the project. A number of young people from the WATS project would choose Town University if they went on to higher education. The male project worker felt quite sure this would not have happened if they had not participated on the WATS project.

Their knowledge of possible routes to take within further and higher education was also increased through their exposure to a university campus. Many of the young people now understand the career options that exist within the area of sport in particular. Being exposed to qualified coaches, and undertaking a community coaching qualification, had contributed to this awareness. The "real life" situation of the female participants however means that choosing sport as a possible career path was unlikely. Many of the young Muslim women knew that their parents would not necessarily encourage sport as a career route because of cultural restrictions; the young women would however consider coaching voluntarily to "give something back" to the community.

The personal benefits of the project, especially for the young Muslim women, cannot be underestimated. Many expressed the view that the project had given them the chance to socialise outside of school. Many of the females commented that they rarely spent their free time outside of the family home. They were not expected by their families to be out of their home in the evenings or at weekends; this contrasted with the male participants, who generally had more freedom and often spend time outside the family home with friends. With much of the females' leisure time usually spent in the home, the opportunities offered by the WATS project were something they simply hadn't had before.

> "I don't really socialise that much outside of school, a lot of my friends I see them at school and I don't really see them after that … it's like good to see your friends … it is just a good experience." [*Female Participant*]

> "As well as taking part in sports you are meeting up with friends aren't you, you are doing something useful with your time." [*Female Participant*]

The benefits of participating in the WATS project for the young women were clear. Increased self-esteem and confidence were two benefits mentioned by nearly every female WATS participant. The personal development course undertaken alongside the sport sessions had given the young people the confidence to discuss personal issues, to identify and address their strengths and weaknesses, to stand up and present information to a group, and to openly discuss their religion and culture. The main reason behind this new found confidence was that the young participants felt comfortable. This was assured by providing the young people with a comfortable environment, which met their needs, and having sessions led by a person who was from their own community.

Conclusion

This paper is based on research with young people from the Muslim community within Town. Although some of the issues raised here may be specific to that community, others have merged which have a wider relevance.

Foremost amongst those are the points raised, in both phases of the research, about the appropriate forms of provision for minority groups.

The importance of having someone from the targeted community to work on the project's behalf was a crucial aspect of WATS. This issue was highlighted to us during the interviews with professional and voluntary workers, and when the project was operating it proved be the most important factor affecting the success of the targeted provision. Similarly, at both stages of the research, family influence was confirmed as important. Gaining access to, and the trust of, parents was central to ensuring the young people participated on the project. The community insider helped gain the trust of the parents by meeting with them, discussing what the project was about, and ensuring them that their son or daughter was entering a safe environment. And finally the environment and 'meeting of needs' was also crucial to the project. Because the needs of the young people were met, the environment was safe and welcoming, their participation was nearly always guaranteed. Making the environment suitable and welcoming was particularly important when trying to encourage the young Muslim women to participate.

Addressing these issues allowed the WATS project to have reasonable success in attracting and retaining participants. The response of the female participants was particularly positive. In due course it became clear that WATS participants had increased their own understanding of further and higher education through regularly attending events at Town University. It was not expected that this would lead to immediate increases in entries to further and higher education participation: few of the participants are of the appropriate age and this effect needs to be monitored over a longer period of time. The indications are, however, that appropriately delivered, sport can be a useful tool in engaging with young people with the aim of tackling educational dimensions of social exclusion.

We would conclude, however, by suggesting that the impact of projects such as WATS should not be measured solely in terms of progress towards measurable policy goals. The young Muslim women who have participated on the WATS project have experienced many benefits: the project has not only increased opportunities for them to be physically active in sport, but has provided them with a safe and acceptable social space for socialising with each other. While these "personal benefits" were not part of the specified aims of the project, they are relevant to notions of inclusion that embrace empowerment of individuals. The value attached by the girls to the opportunities to be together and explore, share and develop their ethnicity suggests that the project may also have contributed to their sense of identity and to their cohesion as a community-within-a-community. Their exposure to us, and ours to them, have certainly strengthened our mutual understanding and collaborations. These are very positive indicators of the potential value of sport to contribute to the underlying social processes of inclusion. We look forward to exploring them in greater depth in subsequent analyses.

References

Coalter, F., Allison, M., & Taylor, J. (2000) *The role of sport in regenerating deprived urban areas.* Edinburgh: Scottish Executive Central Research Unit.

Collins, F., Henry, I., Houlihan, B. and Buller, J. (1999) *Research report: Sport and social exclusion,* A report to the Department of Culture, Media and Sport.

Department for Culture, Media and Sport. (1999 *Policy Action Team 10: A report to the Social Exclusion Unit.* London: UK.

Department for Education and Skills. (2004). *www.dfes.gov.uk;* accessed 27.08.04

Department for Education and Skills: *Five Year Strategy for Children and Learners.* Presented to Parliament by the Secretary of State for Education and Skills. July, 2004.

Higher Education Funding Council for England (2004) *www.hefce.ac.uk;* accessed Aug. 28, 2004.

Kay, T.A. and Lowrey, J. (2003) *Interesting times ahead: The potential of sport for encouraging access to higher education by young people from ethnic minorities.* Report to the Higher Education Funding Council for England, Loughborough: Loughborough University

Long, J., Welch, M., Bramham, P., Butterfield, J., Hylton, K., Lloyd, E. (2002) *Count me in: The dimensions of social inclusion through culture and sport.* Leeds: Centre for Leisure and Sport Research

Papworth, R. M. (2001) *Charnwood Borough Economic Profile.* Leicestershire County Council.

Social Exclusion Unit (1999) *Bridging the gap: New opportunities for 16-18 year olds not in education, employment or training.*

The Future of Higher Education: Presented by the Secretary of State for Education and Skills. January, 2003.

THE VOICE OF THE FAMILY: INFLUENCES ON MUSLIM GIRLS' RESPONSES TO SPORT

Tess Kay

Institute of Youth Sport, Loughborough University

Introduction

One of the more welcome features of the 'New Labour' years has been the move towards evidence-based social policy. In the context of sports policy, this has produced a number of searching analyses (e.g. Coalter *et al.*, 2000; Collins *et al.*, 1999; Long *et al.*, 2002) of the contribution that sport can make to a range of social outcomes, most notably those contributing to social inclusion. On balance these reviews suggest that while in theory, sport may have considerable potential benefits to offer, in practice few of these have been proven.

Despite this, conviction about the capacity of sport to contribute to social change has fuelled a wide range of sports-based initiatives directed at diverse groups from varied social and cultural circumstances. Most of these have focussed on young people who are a primary target for policies to address social exclusion in relation to the dimensions of educational attainment, improved health and reduced youth crime. Many of these projects have ambitious aims: their objectives lie beyond sports participation, to effecting change in young people's lives. It is these more ambitious aims — and the claims that go with them — that give sports researchers pause.

This paper offers a contribution to these debates through an investigation of the response of young Muslim women from a Midlands community to a sports-based Widening Participation (WP) initiative designed to promote post-school education. The two-year project, funded by the European Social Fund to run from January 2002, offered an integrated programme of sport and educational activities designed to attract young people from local ethnic communities. Activities were offered on site at the educational institutions involved, to encourage participants to become familiar with and comfortable in FE/HE settings. The purpose of the associated research programme was to generate understanding of the responses of the participants to provision, and to do so at a number of levels. At the 'administrative' (Yule, 1992) level, the requirement was for a fairly conventional evaluation exercise that could inform scheme management and funding agencies about the operation of the scheme (Lowrey and Kay, 2005, this volume). However, the nature and organisation of the project, and the researchers' position relative to it, offered additional opportunities to undertake more fundamental exploration of the lives of the young women participants. It is on this deeper level of analysis that this paper focuses.

The research reported here is an initial and small-scale attempt to locate responses to sports policy initiatives within the context of broader lifestyles. In this instance those under study are young Muslim women currently living in Britain and conducting their day-to-day lives in the context of varied and sometimes contradictory influences of their religion, the culture of their family's country of origin, and their exposure to western values and expectations. This paper tries to illuminate these processes, by using sport as a vehicle for deconstructing these elements of the young women's experiences. The paper is not, therefore, only concerned with understanding how 'being a Muslim young woman in Britain' may affect sport, but also seeks to show how analysis through sport may contribute to our understanding of being a young British Muslim woman.

The key theme within this analysis is specific consideration of the significance of 'family'. Much has of course been written about the distinctive lifestyles of British Muslims in comparison to the majority population (e.g. Beishon, Modood and Virdee, 1998; Berthoud, 2000; Elliott, 1996; Husain and O'Brien, 2001; Modood, Berthoud, Lakey, Nazroo, Smith, Verdee and Beishon, 1997; Pilkington, 2003). Particular attention has also been paid to the special impact that religious and cultural expectations have on Muslim females (e.g. Menski, 1999; Bhopal, 1999). All of these accounts acknowledge the influence of 'family' and emphasise the contrasting status of family in comparison to its position within white British society, and the particular strength of this influence on the behaviour of young women. It is crucial, therefore, that analyses of sport also address this dimension. This paper does so in some detail, explicitly considering the nature of the influence exerted by 'the voice of the family' on young Muslim women's involvement in sport.

The research context: being Muslim in Britain

Increasing cultural diversity in Britain is fuelling a growing policy and academic literature examining the situation and experiences of members of minority populations. Analyses range from large-scale quantitative and in-depth qualitative empirical accounts to conceptual and theoretical discussions about the relationship between culture, ethnicity and identity. This necessarily brief review considers the broad shift in conceptual underpinning of studies of minority ethnic groups, before examining in greater detail the nature of 'family' in the lives of British Muslims.

Understanding ethnicity

In recent years there has been a shift in frameworks for researching issues relating to race and ethnicity. These have moved from a concept of 'race' that is essentially rooted in biological difference and distinguished by physical appearance (especially skin colour), to a more complex notion of 'ethnicity' that embodies ancestry, history and culture and is socially constructed. The latter approach emphasises diversity among minority ethnic groups and recognises that "socio-economic positions and identities of their members are not structurally determined but are (at least partially) formed by their actions" (Pilkington, 2003: p. 2). Individuals and communities thus actively engage in the process of identity negotiation and ethnic identities are therefore dynamic and fluid (Pilkington, 2003: p. 7).

These conceptions have implications for our understanding of the experiences of minority populations. The early 'host-immigrant thesis', current in Britain during the relatively large immigrations of 1950s–70s, saw the host society as culturally homogeneous and immigrants as bearers of an 'alien' (and potentially 'disruptive'), culture (Elliott, 1996: p. 41). The assumption was that in the long term the immigrant population would relinquish their own values and adopt those of the host. This expectation of 'assimilation' has become outmoded in the face of growing evidence that minority populations preserve their traditions and draw on the cultural capital of their own communities. The Runnymede Trust's millennium Parekh Report (2000) encapsulated current ideas of multi-culturalism in its exploration of 'the future of multi-ethnic Britain'. In other words, rather than experiencing a move to cultural homogeneity, we are witnessing cultural diversity both between the white majority population and non-white groups, and between different minority ethnic communities.

Elliott (1996) has argued that the most significant manifestation of this diversity is in family life. She places family very centrally at the heart of cultural identity and depicts different family arrangements and values as crucial distinguishing characteristics of different ethnic groups. In this her conclusions are similar to those drawn by Bhopal (1999), whose research into women in east London found that a majority valued South Asian family traditions, including the practice of arranged marriages, precisely because they represented something distinctive about South Asian personal and collective cultural identity. Harvey's (2001) compilation of analyses of the mechanisms by which minority families in four different countries interact with dominant cultures similarly emphasised the importance attached to 'maintaining our differences': in fact this theme was so dominant that it became the title for this edited collection. Berthoud, too, in his analytical account of family formation in multi-cultural Britain, claims that "it is diversity between minority groups which is their most striking characteristic" and that "nowhere is this diversity more apparent than in family structures" (Berthoud, 2000: p. 2). Reflecting on similar findings, Beishon Modood and Virdee (1998) have argued that because of the value attached to this variety of family forms, multiculturalism 'has to support a diversity in partnering and parenting'.

There is, however, potential for tensions to arise when minority groups interact with a host culture with very different familial values. In relation to this Elliott suggests that while minority ethnic groups do modify their traditional family arrangements as a result of interplay with the majority culture, they do so in ways that are consistent with their own traditions (Elliott, 1996: 41). This concurs with Pilkington's (2003) view that minorities draw on their own extensive cultural capital in establishing their identity in western contexts. Berthoud's analysis, drawing on multiple sources, suggested that three quite distinct family patterns were evident among different population groups; however, despite these marked contrasts, all three were in fact 'moving in the same direction', away from 'traditional 'family values. With appropriate caveats, he described Caribbeans in Britain as being ahead of the trend in the white population and South Asians as being behind it (Berthoud: 2000). 'Family' is thus a central site for exploration of the significance of interaction between minority and majority groups in the construction of individual and collective identity.

The primacy of 'family' in defining ethnic groups is of particular significance for women. Many of the most visible distinguishing characteristics of the family arrangements of minorities lie in the roles ascribed to female members of the family. In Britain today, the most conspicuous manifestation of this is among those Muslim families of South Asian origin that follow a traditional interpretation of Islam (Elliot, 1996). As Walseth and Fasting (2003) highlight, the Islamic faith is variously interpreted. Throughout the west, and to a much lesser extent within the Islamic nations, many Muslims follow a 'progressive' interpretation of Islam, and this is reflected, for example, by the presence of Muslim women in public life and in westernised dress. Berthoud (2000) has shown, however, that when Muslims in Britain do adhere to a tradtional interpretation of Islam, their family arrangements are more different from the majority white population than those of any other minority ethnic group.

The next section examines this in more detail, as the context within which young Muslim women construct their identity and day-to-day lives.

Family ideologies among Muslim South Asians

Analysis of contemporary family life among minority ethnic groups has to be rooted in understanding of the legacy of values that are brought to bear on 'family' in these communities. In the case of Muslims of South Asian origin, these stem from the closely intertwining of culture and religion. In the popular view it is likely that these two are conflated, and that culturally determined practices such as arranged marriages are assumed to have their origins in Islamic teaching. Although to a considerable extent South Asian culture and Islam are mutually reinforcing, this is not universally the case: some Muslims, sensitive to western criticisms of their faith, will be at pains to emphasise that the tradition of arranged marriages, for example, does not originate in the teachings of Islam. In some circumstances this discrepancy between religion and culture can provide some 'room to manoeuvre', especially for young people. For the outsider, however, it can make it difficult to disentangle the relative influence of culture and religious teachings.

This is complicated by the all-embracing nature of Islam. As Verma and Darby explain, there is no separation of religious and secular activities in Islam: 'for a Muslim, religion, law and social organisation are combined, so that injunctions extend beyond religious practices to aspects of conduct which, in Western society, are regulated (if at all) by secular law and civil authority' (Verma and Darby, 1994: p. 42). Islam also differs from some other faiths, including Christianity, in the permanence attributed to its teachings: "while Christianity has a tradition of progression, change and re-evaluation,

Islam has no such tradition. On the contrary, the truths of the Koran are seen as immutable". This has implications for those who formulate their personalities in 'Koranic terms' (Verma and Darby, 1994: p. 43).

Islamic teachings about marriage and the roles of men and women are critical components of distinctive South Asian Muslim lifestyles in Britain. The dominant ideologies of family in many British Muslim communities derive, however, not from their common religion but from the traditions of South Asia. This cultural legacy has been most fully described in Ballard's (1982) account of family life to which contemporary writers continue to refer. This outlined 'the basic patterns and principles of family organization which are characteristic of virtually every community of Indian, Pakistani and Bangladeshi origin in Britain'. Ballard's description is illuminating in highlighting two distinctive features: the gendered structure of family, and its 'collective' or 'corporate' nature. His account captures the privileged position of males as the family's defining members particularly clearly, explaining how the membership of a family unit consisted of a man, his sons and grandsons, together with their wives and unmarried daughters. In other words, female children of a family were not permanent members of their parents' household: only sons had full rights of inheritance and remained family members all their lives. At marriage daughters left their natal home and became members of their husbands' family. On the other hand, and in sharp contrast to English families in both modern and historical times, there was no expectation that sons should establish independent households of their own at marriage (Ballard, 1982: p. 3).

The second central feature of South Asian family life is its corporate nature. This is one of the most striking contrasts with western notions of marriage relationships as intimate partnerships between two people and based on romantic love. In contrast, Ballard describes South Asian families as ideologically focussed on the family group with little regard for individual freedom or self-interest. Verma and Darby (1994), writing about the British Bangladeshi community in the 1990s, describe it as 'essentially collectivist': "that is to say that its members perceive themselves not as individuals but also as members of a group — the family" (1994: p. 45). Bhopal captures this well in her description of marriage as "an arrangement between two families, not two individuals" (Bhopal, 1999: p. 120).

An important point to consider in relation to the collective nature of the family is the positioning of the family within its community. Many westerners have some awareness that the notion of family honour ('izzat') is central to ethnic groups of South Asian origin. The collective efforts of the individual members of the family are therefore directed at both maintaining and increasing izzat. The maintenance of izzat depends on the family's' wealth and on its members' conformity with ideal norms of behaviour; however, the most effective way for families to *increase* it is through arranging prestigious marriage matches for the families' daughters. As Bhopal points out, this means it is women who are ultimately responsible for izzat: "if a daughter steps out of line, she not only jeopardises her own respect in the community but her parents' social standing" (1999: p. 121).

It is against the backdrop of these traditions that young Muslim South Asian women in Britain are constructing their identities. Knowledge of the legacy of their family's country of origin is thus an important component in understanding their experiences as they do so. It is perhaps more important, however, to examine how their parents' generation has maintained or deviated from this heritage as they have reconstructed family life in multi-cultural Britain.

Muslim South Asian families in contemporary Britain

The 2001 Census revealed that the United Kingdom had become more culturally diverse than ever before (National Statistics, 2004). The non-white population had risen by 53% in 10 years to number over 4.6 million individuals who made up just under 8% of the total population. Adults and children of Asian/British Asian ethnicity made up fractionally more than half (50.3%) of the non-white population, compared to 25% Black/Black British and 15% of mixed origin (National Statistics, 2004: p. 2)

In social, demographic and economic terms the Asian/British Asian sub-group differed from population averages in a number of respects: their age profile was younger, their economic activity was lower, and compared to other groups, they had an above-average risk of low-income and poverty. Negative experiences were particularly common among Asian/British Asian people whose families were of South Asian (Pakistan or Bangladeshi) origin, who were least likely to be in employment and most likely to be dependent on social assistance payments (National Statistics, 2004).

Some of the most conspicuous differences between ethnic groups, however, related to family living arrangements. Here again Asians/British Asians of South Asian origin stood out. They presented a very different pattern from the white population and differed even more from those classed as Black /Black British. Census 2001 data showed that South Asians of Pakistani or Bangladeshi origin were most likely to be married, most likely to live in households with dependent children, and on average lived in households significantly larger than the population as a whole (National Statistics 2004: p. 11). They were also least likely to live in a lone parent household, more likely than the white population to live in houses shared by more than one family with dependent children, and much less likely to have a household member in care. Statistically, some of these differences were very large: Bangladeshi (average 4.5 persons) and Pakistani households (4.1) were on average almost twice as large as white households (average 2.3). Bangladeshi households were also nearly three times as likely to contain at least one dependent child (74%) and Pakistani households more than twice as likely to (66%) as white households (28%).

Qualitative research sponsored by the Joseph Rowntree Foundation (JRF) explored the values and attitudes underpinning particular patterns of family life among different ethnic groups in Britain (Beishon, Modood and Virdee, 1998). Pakistanis and Bangladeshis emerged as the 'most traditional': the majority believing in multi-generational households with parents and their adult sons' families, and any unmarried children, living together. The current parent generation in particular saw multi-generational households as an ideal living arrangement that fostered meaningful relationships within the family. Younger Pakistani and Bangladeshi adults were generally as much in favour of living in an extended family, although a few felt it was better to have parents living locally rather than with the household, for reasons of privacy and autonomy.

One of the findings to emerge from the JRF study was the importance attached by South Asian households to religion. Parents of Pakistani or Bangladeshi origin were the most concerned that their children should be involved in some form of cultural or religious activity and have access to Islamic teaching. They were also generally against marrying outside their ethnic group, although this might be acceptable if the prospective partner was Muslim or prepared to become a Muslim. Overall, interviewees of South Asian origin saw their families as very different from white families, and were critical of white parents' perceived lack of commitment to parenting, which they saw as fostering indiscipline and lack of respect among the young for their parents and elders.

However, while the overall picture conformed to the idea of Asian households in Britain reflecting 'traditional' family structures, there have been other indications of a more complex picture. Although Berthoud (2000) found that Pakistani and Bangladeshi were clearly the most conservative of ethnic groups in the population, even here there were indicators of change. Firstly, many British Asians appeared to be moving away from the tradition of arranged marriages, although this development is much less common among Muslims than among Hindus and Sikhs (Berthoud 2000: p. 16). Secondly, although a clear majority of Pakistani and Bangladeshi women looked after their home and family full-time, this was becoming less common among the growing number of women who are obtaining good educational qualifications. Thirdly and possibly associated with this shift in female career expectations, although Pakistani and Bangladeshi women have very high fertility rates from their teenage years to their early forties, there were clear signs of a reduction in the number of children being born to women from these communities.

The changes Berthoud describes centre mainly on shifts in the life patterns of women. Dale, Shaheen, Kaira and Fieldhouse (2002) throw more light on this, particularly in relation to changing patterns of education among Muslim females. They note that when the first generation of Pakistani and Bangladeshi women arrived in Britain, their lack of qualifications and limited fluency in English were major barriers to employment. Subsequently, young Pakistani and Bangladeshi women educated in the UK have had the opportunity to acquire language and qualifications that was not available to their mothers, and most have also been exposed to Western cultural values as well as the traditional Muslim values of their parents and family (Dale *et al.*, 2002: p. 943). Berthoud reinforces this, pointing out that while the fourth PSI survey found that a clear majority of Pakistani (70%) and Bangladeshi (81%) wives were full-time homemakers, Labour Force Survey data demonstrates a strong correlation between levels of qualification and employment status. Thus, while unqualified Muslim wives of the current parent generation were unlikely to take up low-status employment, there is a "strong implication" that "more Muslim women will find their way into the labour market as more of them obtain educational qualifications" (Berthoud, 2000: p. 18).

These changes in family life and educational experiences place Muslim young women in the vanguard of changing South Asian ethnic identities in Britain. When changes in family patterns are combined with changing expectations of education and employment, it becomes evident that there may be many points of divergence and possible conflict between young girls and their parents. It would be simplistic, however, to see these developments as one-directional. In the earlier discussion of multiculturalism, the importance of acknowledging the positive importance attached to these distinctive traditions was emphasised. It is in this context of complex and almost contradictory influences that the current study is located.

The study

The current research was conducted in collaboration with a 'widening participation' initiative targeting local young people from minority ethnic communities in a Midlands town in England, UK. The project, 'Widening Access Through Sport' (WATS) was funded by the European Social Fund to run for two years from January 2003 and was part of a broader agenda in Europe to increase levels of education and training among young people.

The WATS project aimed to engage young people aged 14–19 from minority ethnic communities in a programme of sport and educational activities designed to encourage them to continue their education beyond the age of compulsory schooling. Particular emphasis was to be given to working over an extended period with relatively small groups of young people, and delivering activity programmes designed around their specific needs and interests. In adopting this approach, the project was building on a preceding initiative, the 'Higher Education Participation Through Sport' project, which had indicated the potential of sport as a medium for work of this type (Kay and Lowrey, 2003).

At the time of the research in March 2004, three 'education and sport' development workers had been appointed to the project. One of these was working with a variety of ethnic groups in City, while the remaining two were based in nearby Town where they were employed to run separate activity programmes for male and female Muslim youth. The activity programme aimed at Muslim young women was proving to be particularly successful (see also Lowrey and Kay, 2005, this volume), attracting regular and continuous attendance. Informal feedback from participants and the activity leader indicated a high level of enjoyment and satisfaction among the young women taking part.

Despite the successes, there were some difficulties in the arrangements. The Muslim young women's elements of the project were often the most difficult to organize in practical terms because of their requirement for female-only activity areas from which males could be excluded. As researchers we also became aware that there were occasions when the young women were only allowed to take part after the activity leader had visited their home and explained the activities in detail to the parents, and assured them that the arrangements and facilities met the requirements of Islam. At the same time, the girls themselves were confounding our expectations: they were far more responsive to the sports elements of the programme than we anticipated, to the extent of moving quickly from personal participation to taking entry-level coaching qualifications. To a westernized outsider, the assertiveness and energy they displayed appeared at odds with the constraints surrounding them. We became interested in these apparent contradictions and in the role of the girls' families in influencing them.

Our involvement in the project, as researchers and project managers, offered the opportunity to investigate this. We were able to establish a small-scale in-depth research project in which the girls were actively involved at all stages of the research process. The first-level aim of the research was to identify the influence of the girls' families on their daughters' involvement in the WATS project. Within this, however, the project was also an effective vehicle for exploring parental expectations of young Muslim females in relation to education, employment and domesticity, and to compare those with the girls' own responses to these issues. These issues are the main focus of this paper.

Methods

The study was conducted as an education and personal development element within the girls' activity programme during the Easter school holiday. Three key principles underlay the approach:

1. that the girls should have maximum influence in defining the parameters of the research through their input into the detailed design of the interview schedule;

2. that the format of the research would allow us to access a group with whom we had had no direct contact and with whom we might have limited credibility, but who were likely to be more responsive to their own children; and

3. that the girls would be fully involved in the interpretation and analysis of the outcomes of the interviews, and would have opportunity to respond to the findings.

The data collection took the form of a preliminary interview with the development worker to help define the parameters of the study, and a set of in-depth interviews with the girls' parents and other family members, conducted by the girls themselves.

The family interviews addressed three themes — views on the girls' involvement in sport, views on their involvement in education, and expectations of their adult lives and domestic roles.

Under the guidance of the researchers and the sport and education development worker, the girls met as a group on four occasions over a two-week period, and between meetings undertook some additional independent work. The format was:

1. Workshop 1: Introductory workshop introducing the girls to the idea of social science research, and explaining the researchers' interest in the role the girls' families play in their lives. Group exercise discussing the issues to be addressed. Girls work in small sub-groups to draw up lists of questions to be asked of parents. They also completed a background questionnaire about their family, including details of family members, their employment status, and their English language usage and competence in different situations (written, spoken etc).

2. Researchers collate information from the girls and compile interview schedule using their questions. No question topics are rejected although wording on some is edited and like questions are combined.

3. Workshop 2: researchers present the completed interview schedule to the girls. Girls are trained to use mini-disc recorders to conduct interviews. They practice interviewing each other including recording the interview.

4. Girls conduct interviews with one family member and begin to transcribe interviews.

5. Workshop 3: girls report-back on the findings of the interviews. The activity leader, a Muslim female, leads the discussion. The workshop discussion is recorded on minidisk. The girls and project/research staff complete the transcription of the interviews.

6. Workshop 4: the activity leader leads a second discussion on the interviews, this time focusing on the girls' response to their parents' views, and their own attitudes to the issues covered. The workshop discussion is recorded on mini-disc.

This methodological approach raises a range of complex issues and a fuller account of these is to be given in Kay 2005 (forthcoming). In many respects the traditional role of the researcher was devolved to the development worker, who undertook the focus group discussions with the girls. The reiterative structure of the data collection then allowed comparisons to be made between the views of the parents and the views of the girls, and also allowed the girls' explanations for differences between the two to be considered.

Results

Research participants and their families

The research study was conducted with 7 Muslim girls, aged 13 — 18. At the time of the research all were in full-time education at local schools/colleges. They varied in ethnicity, describing themselves as white and black Africans, Bangladeshi and Arab.

Six of the seven girls wore the headscarf, indicating conformance with a fairly traditional interpretation of Islam.

Two of the girls were sisters so the number of families involved in the research was 6. The girls' parents were first generation immigrants to Britain and their households were two-generational: some were 'large' households, but not all. Most of their parents (8/12) were not in employment — 3 fathers and 5 mothers; of the remainder, 2 were employed part-time and 2 full-time. Parents varied in their ease of use of English, which was not always the first language used at home, and a number of parents were considered by their daughters to experience some difficulty in using either written or spoken English, or both. The combination of low employment and (some) English language difficulties indicated that this group might experience a degree of separation from the local majority population. Such separation may encourage strong internal community ties, and also represents an important difference between the experiences of the parent generation and those of their children. In contrast to their parents, the girls involved in the study were fully competent in English, and through their schooling had regular contact with young white people and those from other ethnic groups.

Family voices on Muslim girls participating in sport

Islam does not forbid its female followers to participate in sport: on the contrary, taking care of the body through exercise is seen as a duty and participating in sport is condoned for this reason. Constraints do however arise from the circumstances in which girls and women can participate, for unless they are wholly concealed from the male gaze, girls participating in sport will infringe the religious requirement and cultural expectation of modesty in females. As we have seen, this has social consequences in that a daughter behaving in an unseemly way will damage family izzat.

The family 'voice' on participating in sport reflected these contrasting issues, expressing both approval and constraint. There was outright support for girls participating: in one sibling interview, a brother went so far as to say that 'Muslim girls just don't do enough sport' and criticised them for not doing more. The parent generation was also supportive, including mothers who had not been able to participate themselves under the more traditional restrictions of their generation and now wished to see their daughters enjoy a wider range of experiences. Family members also referred to the fact that taking part in sport conformed to Islam, and supported participation for this reason.

The family voice of constraint was also in evidence. Throughout the interviews, those who expressed support for sport stressed that this was only acceptable if the conditions conformed to Islam. If parents were uncertain about the suitability of the occasion and facilities, they could prevent their daughter attending. One of the female participants referred to a friend who was not allowed to take part in the project, while another recognised that the decision about her own and her friends' attendance rested wholly with parents:

> "She did tell me at school that she likes taking part in sport but her parents don't have that understanding so… they object to her coming along."

> "You have to realise that if the parents are going to say no…that is it, and you will just have to leave them with that choice."

The girls themselves embraced sport enthusiastically. They were particularly responsive to the elements of the project which had embedded education within sporting activities, e.g. through the coaching courses undertaken. Sport appeared to have been very effectively integrated into these elements of the activity programme:

> "You know that coaching thing that we did, I was thinking, god it has got so much to it."

> "When you think of sports like hockey you think of playing the game but there is more to it, links with sociology and everything else."

> "Yes I thought how much do you need to study to be a coach."

Islam places a strong value on education as a matter of self-development and much of the WATS project 'syllabus' developed for this group focused on these matters. Here, too, sport appeared to contribute:

> "I have gained more knowledge on sports, [it is] not just something that you practically take part in, it is communicating with each other, learning to respect one another, helping one another, building your self-confidence and esteem."

The situation in relation to sport, therefore, was mixed. Family members were supportive, but the proviso was that sport must conform to acceptable behaviour for young women. This conformance was partly a matter of religious observance, but also one of social respectability. The family was a conduit for both these sets of values.

Family voices on Muslim girls taking part in educational activities

Levels of progression to further and higher education by young Muslims in Britain are low. A number of researchers have explained this in terms of the relative poverty of much of the Muslim community in Britain (Modood *et al.*, 1997; Parekh, 2000) and the need for young people to leave education to work and supplement family income from a young age. Our own research into the HEPTS project, the precursor to WATS, indicated that many young people from the Bangladeshi community in Town were leaving school at the minimum legal age for precisely this reason — to earn an immediate and necessary income for their families (Kay and Lowrey, 2003). In many cases it therefore appeared to be practical circumstances rather than attitudinal factors that limit educational progression. In other words, the under-representation of young Muslims in post-school education belies the extreme importance attached to education within Islam.

The value attached to education was central to the activities programme provided by the WATS project for the Muslim girls' participant group. The Muslim female development worker was key in developing the programme to deliver a substantial educational syllabus, reflecting her certainty that families would be supportive of girls participating in educational activities.

The research amply justified this assumption. The value attached to education was so entrenched that one older sibling found it almost incomprehensible to be asked to explain this:

> "Education is important, it can't be overstated. You are asking me to explain the obvious".

Family approval of education for girls was expressed in terms of conforming to Islam, and also in relation to material circumstances. Parents believed from their own experiences that educational qualifications were needed for financial security.

However, more mixed views came to the fore when family members were asked about the suitability of further and higher education for the girls. Again, the views expressed related to Islam: how could the girls pursue education in an environment where they would be particularly exposed to western culture, and separated from their families and thus insulated from their guiding influence? An additional factor arose in relation to the role which education and employment might play in the girls' adult lives. Having a 'career' was very definitely seen as a secondary consideration, and even an inappropriate one. Although education was valued for girls in their current situation, therefore, there were reservations about where it might lead.

The girls themselves held similarly contradictory views. On the one hand, they valued education and also expressed some resentment of the constraints they faced in comparison to their male counterparts:

[1] "Education I think it is important for a girl."

[2] "I don't think it is fair that the guy can go off to uni no problem whatsoever and the girl on the other hand has to stay at home and be the good one."

The girls' discussion of education was also revealing for what it displayed about their uncertainties and how they intended to resolve them. The following exchange was an illuminating cameo, illustrating the ambiguities that sometimes surrounded the requirements of Islam, and providing an example of how the girls would actively seek out guidance on how to conform to these:

[3] "Well it has something to do with modesty doesn't it.... It's safer for girls to stay within the home... Islam has set down these laws, you can't travel 46–48 miles without..."

[1] "But it says no matter where education is, then there is nothing wrong with that."

Development worker: "With universities I am not sure, you would have to put it to a scholar and see what they say."

As well as being concerned about conforming to Islam, the girls were concerned at a more personal level about with how the experience of being at an educational institution might affect them. They had a very strong awareness of the issues of being exposed to western culture.

[1] "I would be worried that I would commit more sin if I moved away."

[2] "I actually agree with everything my mum said. The main thing was she said you can get influenced — and you can get influenced very easily. I would probably be scared to go on and even do A levels and stuff."

[3] "You'd be scared to do A levels? You'd be at college and everything."

[2] "But you'd have free periods and stuff...."

[3] "Are you easily influenced?"

[1] "She is..."

The findings concerning 'education' raise a number of issues. While there is no question about the support in principle for Muslim girls and young women engaging in educational activities, there are, however, potential conflicts with religious and cultural requirements. It is interesting to see how these conflicts are experienced and articulated by the girls themselves. While there is some expression of dissatisfaction with the different freedoms ascribed to males and females, there is also considerable acceptance of the constraints that underlie this. The girls explicitly expressed fears about their own potential behaviour and their possible deviation from Islam. Perhaps of most interest, however, are the expressions of how the girls engage with the identity work required to resolve these dilemmas. This small group have recourse to specific teachings/guidance from religious leaders. Within the discourse surrounding Muslim girls' identity in Britain, there is a discernible discourse of 'what am I allowed to be?' The very specific sources of guidance available on this position were rather different for these girls than from many other British youth.

Family voices on adult roles

Family attitudes to girls' involvement in education were closely linked to views about the adult pathways that Muslim girls would take. Parental comments reflected both the power of tradition, and the pressure for change. For the most part, the girls' reported that their parents — mothers especially — emphasised the role of mother as the primary one:

"My mum said education is important but being a mother is more important than education."

Some mothers were, however, keen that their daughters should have wider experiences, and showed some acceptance of women's ambition beyond the home:

"She said whatever I want to become I have to achieve it through education. So she said, [I should] try to achieve my goal and aim high."

The girls themselves displayed both attitudes. They valued motherhood:

[1] "I think being a mother is more important than having a career. My mum thinks being a mum is more important."
[2] "It is kind of like a career..."
[3] "...being a full-time mum."

There were nonetheless aspects of the traditional South Asian Muslim woman's role from which some wanted to distance themselves. The discussion of adult roles brought up the fundamental issue of girls' relationship to their family and the tension between the closeness of this relationship and any individual desire for independence:

"But I don't like to be scared of doing something... I want to be independent and think for myself. If you are always under your parents' guidance you don't always think for yourself do you, you can't really be your own person....It is also I don't like when you are asked to make a decision and you're like, what shall I do, I'll go and ask my dad...I'd be calling them up when I was 50 or something... I'd rather think for myself."

Discussion: difference and identity

This paper investigated responses to sports-based inclusion initiatives. Its focus was very specific — on Muslim young women, participating in a targeted activity programme designed to increase progression to post-compulsory education. It was intended, however, that the scope of the research would allow exploration of broader issues of the target group's experiences as second-generation Muslim females in Britain. This it did, yielding data not only on the three central themes of sport, education and adult roles, but also on the minutiae of everyday life.

The picture that emerged of how the girls lived their lives as members of their parents' household illustrated the prominence of 'family' in their day-to-day lives. It also highlighted elements of the girls' experiences that represented 'difference' in comparison to the westernised lifestyles of the majority of the local population. Two examples of this were particularly in evidence. Firstly, the research revealed something about the *extent* of family. A number of the girls came from large families — as did the WATS development worker, who was one of 9 siblings. In addition to this, however, families who had been living in Town for more than a generation were usually related to other families living locally. In these cases, the number of people to whom any individual was related could be very high. The development worker estimated that she was related to around 65 people living in Town and in the questionnaire completed at the outset of the research, three of the girls estimated that they had between 40–60 relatives living there. As members of the Muslim community tended to live in properties located near to each other, this could be very close proximity indeed. For the girls, this meant that there was an extensive number of people with an interest in their behaviour. This echoes a point made by Singleton and Green (2004, this volume), about the sense of surveillance that young women can have in these close-knit communities in which cultural norms make the behaviour of young females a particular focus.

Secondly, the research revealed some interesting examples of the relatively constrained spatial scope of the girls' activities. In comparison to non-Muslim teenagers, they spent a high proportion of time in the home and travelled a limited distance beyond it. Even the development worker — an assertive and highly skilled 25 year-old graduate in full-time employment — described her life outside the home as taking place only in work hours: when she returned home at the end of each afternoon, she was expected to remain in the house until re-emerging for work next morning. For the girls, this applied when they returned home from school. This pattern partly reflected the expectation that girls would contribute domestically to the household, and partly concern about the activities they might engage in outside it. Beyond the home, the girls did not travel independently: when, in the course of the project, the development worker took the girls to nearby City 12 miles away, it was the first time that they had spent some time in the city centre unaccompanied by their parents. Their lives were therefore more localised than those of young people from other groups, much more home-based, and involved much less contact with friends and much more time in the company of immediate family.

We have seen previously that maintaining difference in lifestyles is an important component of cultural identity. Although in this study we did not directly question the girls about their notions of 'identity', our intention was to allow evidence of identity work to emerge through explanations of their response to the sports-based scheme. 'Sport' is a useful focus for this type of investigation because of its special position in relation to Muslim women: it is an activity condoned by Islam but severely restricted by cultural restrictions on women. (Hargreaves, 2000) has in fact suggested that in some Islamic states, access to sport has become synonymous with women's broader struggle for gender equity. Questioning Muslim young women about their participation in sport therefore requires them to explicate a broader range of issues relating to their situation.

The study revealed substantial family influence on the response to the sports project by the girls, whose participation was wholly conditional on their parents' approval. However, although authority lay with the parents, there were examples of views being mediated by older siblings, especially older sons. These family members acted as a bridge to the local community from which parents were relatively excluded through their lack of employment and sometimes limited English language skills. In the examples in this study, older siblings' contributions served to increase girls' opportunities rather than constrain them. Some mothers also supported their daughters having something to do beyond the home. There were therefore some indications of family support for a slight widening of opportunities for girls, but still within quite strict limits.

The girls' responses to their families' expectations of their current and adult roles revealed some of the complexities of negotiating identity when positioned between cultures, religions, ethnicities and generations. For the most part the girls were accepting of parental authority and shared their parents' views on appropriate behaviour. Again, however, it was evident that some questioned some of the traditional expectations of them, with some expressions of individualism emerging. While this might indicate a step towards 'modern' values, there was however strong evidence of alternative influences that countered it. Discussions of what was permissible under Islam showed that the girls continually made reference to their faith for guidance on practical matters. Their identity work was concerned, therefore, not just with what they wanted to be, but with establishing what they were 'allowed' to be.

This combination of small indications of movement towards more liberal lifestyles, counterbalanced by explicit reference to Islamic teachings in relation to day-to-day activities, is in accordance with recent analyses that reveal the complexity of ethnicity in Britain. On the one hand, there was evidence of the fluidity described by the Parekh report (2000): parental and sibling attitudes towards the girls' involvement in the project suggested that rather than being "permanently locked into unchanging traditions", the Muslim community in Town was "constantly adapting and diversifying their inherited beliefs and values in the light of the migration experience" (2000: p. 27). The girls were not only experiencing, but also actively creating, a fusion of the traditions of their origins with elements of the majority culture (Modood, Berthoud et al, 1997). This identity work was evident in the girls' dialogues, especially when they confronted uncertainties and differences amongst themselves about what was appropriate and/or required of them as young Muslim women. It was also, however, evident in the voice of the parents, who gave approval to their daughters' involvement in activities which signified change. Some of these changes were modest: for example, participating in sport within a very controlled environment that conforms to Islam is not in itself a major departure. The support for girls' education and higher level qualifications, however, contrasts strongly with their mothers' generation and has the potential to produce more fundamental long-term shifts.

The experiences of the young are an inevitable focus in analyses of these processes of adaptation. Minority ethnic youth have been described as "skilled cross-cultural navigators" (Parekh, 2000: p. 29) who draw not only on their own and the majority culture, but also on the cultures of other minorities in the population. There can be a danger, however, that this navigational process is assumed to be unidirectional — that Muslim youth, for example, are presumed to be moving only towards the progressive elements of other cultures. The findings of this study do not suggest this: rather than abandoning Islam, the girls quite specifically referred to Islam as a source of guidance for how they should conduct their present and adult lives. This very much accords with the work of other writers who have suggested that the 'navigation' process of the younger generation is complex. Modood (1997) talks of young people seeking ways of adapting that accord with their own culture. In the case of Muslims, this means that "new ways of living and the process of gradually becoming a part of British society have to be ultimately justified in terms compatible with a Muslim faith" (Modood, 1997; in Parekh, 2000: p. 31). It is important, therefore, to recognise ethnicity as a source of very positive identity. This may be especially the case among groups which westerners might naively assume have most to 'gain' by casting off their more 'restrictive' traditions. Young women, whose positions in their host culture raise particularly obvious differences with the majority culture, can be especially significant in this. Although South Asian women under scrutiny for maintaining traditions such as arranged marriages may be receptive to a degree of change, they also reject views of their cultures as inferior. Many are active and vocal in criticising aspects of western gender arrangements as more progressive (Barot, Bradley and Fenton, 1999).

Conclusions

This paper sought to contribute to understanding of responses to sports-based activity programmes that support social inclusion policy objectives. It was particularly concerned with locating such responses within broader lifestyles. Looking beyond the particular case study of Muslim young women, at the conceptual level its findings suggest that:

- Research into sports experiences can be effective in yielding understanding of broader social practice. In this respect, sport may be regarded as a valuable tool for deconstructing social phenomena at the micro-level;
- Family context has universal relevance for analyses of sport and leisure behaviour

In conclusion, therefore, 'family' would appear to be an effective, legitimate and productive focus for sports researchers. At present it is also a largely absent one. The focus in this study on family experiences among minority ethnic groups is not intended to imply that family has relevance only in communities where it is acknowledged as a central institution. On the contrary, the message of this research should be that the different positioning of family is an equally important consideration in all cultural contexts. Addressing this may offer us a corrective to the sins of either omitting or over-generalising 'family' in sports research.

References

Ballard, R. (1982) 'South Asian families', in Rapoport, R. N., Fogarty, M. P. and Rapoport, R. (eds) *Families in Britain*. London: Routledge and Kegan Paul.

Barot, R., Bradley, H., and Fenton, S. (1999) *Ethnicity, gender and social change*. London: Macmillan Press Ltd.

Beishon, S., Modood, T. and Virdee, S. (1998) *Ethnic minority families*. London: PSI.

Berthoud, R. (2000) Family formation in multi-cultural Britian: three patterns of diversity. Working paper, Institute for Social and Economic Research, University of Essex.

Bhopal, K. (1999) 'South Asian women and arranged marriages in East London', in Barot, R., Bradley, H., and Fenton, S., *Ethnicity, gender and social change*. London: Macmillan Press Ltd, ch. 6, pp. 117–134.

Coalter, F., Allison, M., & Taylor, J. (2000) *The role of sport in regenerating deprived urban areas*. Edinburgh: Scottish Executive Central Research Unit.

Collins, F., Henry, I., Houlihan, B. and Buller, J. (1999) *Research report: Sport and social exclusion*, A report to the Department of Culture, Media and Sport.

Dale, A., Shaheen, N., Kalra, V. and Fieldhouse, E. (2002) 'Routes into education and employment for young Pakistani and Bangladeshi women in the UK', *Ethnic and Racial Studies*, Vol. 25 no.6: pp. 942–968.

Elliott, F. Robertson (1996) *Gender family and society*. Basingstoke: Macmillan.

Hargreaves, J. (2000) *Heroines of sport: The politics of difference and identity*. London: Routledge.

Harvey, C. (ed) (2001) *Maintaining our differences*. Aldershot: Ashgate.

Husain, F. and O'Brien, M. (2001) 'South Asian Muslims in Britain: Faith, Family and Community', in Harvey, C. (ed) *Maintaining our differences*. Aldershot: Ashgate, pp. 15–28.

Kay, T. A. (2005) 'Research by proxy: Reaching across the divide', *LSA Newsletter* No. 70 (March) Eastbourne: Leisure Studies Association.

Kay, T. A. and Lowrey, J. (2003) *Interesting times ahead: The potential of sport for encouraging access to higher education by young people from ethnic minorities*. Report to the Higher Education Funding Council for England. Loughborough: Loughborough University.

Lowrey, J. and Kay, T. (2005) 'Doing sport, doing inclusion: An analysis of provider and participant perceptions of targeted sport provision for young Muslims', this volume.

Long, J., Welch, M., Bramham, P., Butterfield, J., Hylton, K., Lloyd, E. (2002) *Count me in: The dimensions of social inclusion through culture and sport.* Leeds: Centre for Leisure and Sport Research.

Menski, W. (1999) 'South Asian women in Britain, family integrity and the primary purpose', in Barot, R., Bradley, H., and Fenton, S., *Ethnicity, gender and social change.* London: Macmillan Press Ltd, ch. 4, pp. 81–98.

Modood, T., Berthoud, R., Lakey, J., Nazroo, J., Smith, P., Virdee, S., and Beishon, S. (1997) *Ethnic minorities in Britian.* London: PSI.

National Statistics (2004) *Social focus on ethnicity and identity.* London: HMSO.

Parekh, B. (2000) *The future of multiethnic Britain: The Parekh Report.* London: Profile Books.

Pilkington, A., (2003) *Racial disadvantage and ethnic diversity in Britain.* Basingstoke: Palgrave.

Singleton, C. and Green, E. (2004) '"Safe" spaces: An analysis of the inter-relationships of gender, ethnicity and culture in South Asian women's leisure lives', paper presented at the Leisure Studies Association annual conference, July, Leeds Metropolitan University.

Sport England (1999) *The value of sport.* Sport England, Ref no. 887.

Verma, G. K. and Darby, D. S. (1994) *Winners and losers: ethnic minorities in sport and recreation.* London: Falmer Press.

Walseth, K. and Fasting, K. (2003) 'Islam's view on physical activity and sport: Egyptian women interpreting Islam', *International Review for the Sociology of Sport* 38: pp. 45–60.

Yule, J. (1992) 'Gender and leisure policy', *Leisure Studies* Vol. 11, No. 3: pp. 157–173.

YOUNG PEOPLE, HOLIDAY-TAKING AND CANCER: THE PERCEIVED EFFECTS OF TRAVEL UPON HEALTH AND WELLBEING

Philippa Hunter-Jones

Manchester Metropolitan University

Introduction

This paper reports the empirical findings of a qualitative study undertaken to determine the perceived effects of holiday-taking upon the health and wellbeing of young people treated for cancer. A holiday to Scotland, organised through the Young Oncology Unit (YOU) at Christie Hospital, Manchester UK, a specialist cancer hospital covering the north-west of England, provides the focus for this investigation. The perceived effects identified, found to be consistent with the personal and social learning tasks of adolescence suggested by Hendry *et al.*, (1993), extend beyond the holiday environment contributing in varying ways to personal health; social effectiveness; personal identity; self-image; regaining independence; future career aspirations and socially responsible behaviour.

Background

Illness, particularly serious illness, can generate feelings of vulnerability and emotional dependence. Such feelings are possible at any age, but are likely to be more acute during the adolescent stage given the plethora of changes such an individual has to cope with. Cancer (collective term) is currently the second most common cause of mortality in the UK. Encouragingly, despite the significance of the illness, advances in diagnosis and treatment continue to be achieved. Such advances have prompted new challenges to caring and living with cancer, particularly for those affected at an early age. Yet much of the research considering this has focused upon the effects of cancer upon children (see Eiser, 1993; Faulkner *et al.*, 1995), and only here in a general sense. Consideration of older dependants, twelve to eighteen year olds for instance, is notably sparse.

Leisure-related activities, holiday-taking being one such example, ordinarily should play an important function in the personal development of young people (Coleman and Hendry, 1990; Hendry *et al.*, 1993). Whether this is so for those experiencing ill-health is unclear for whilst considerable evidence exists charting the symbiotic relationship between health and holiday-taking (see for instance Family Holiday Association, 1993; 1996) much of the published work is skewed towards focusing primarily upon the general holiday-taking population. Any consideration of the relationship between ill-health and holiday-taking, in contrast, is notably sparse. Furthermore there is a tendency for the work to cover a broad sample base with the needs of particular market segments such as young people seldom differentiated. Work by the English Tourism Council (ETC) (ETC, 2000) illustrates this shortfall.

Completed during the early part of 2000 and covering 271 General Practitioners' (GPs) in England and a total of 310 across Great Britain as a whole, the ETC (2000) study addressed a number of issues including the effects of holiday-taking upon health and the most beneficial holiday-taking pattern. Whilst acknowledged as contributing to stress, particularly due to financial worries (32%) or the family being 'stuck' together (20%), those in a position to travel were thought likely to seek less medication, make fewer visits to the doctor and take less time off work than those not. In particular, holiday-takers were thought more likely to be relaxed, suffer less stress and be better able to cope with varied life situations and the symptoms of ill-health including depression, insomnia, alcohol and drug dependencies.

Intrinsic benefits acknowledged included prompting opportunities for self-discovery, enriched spirituality and rediscovering a purpose to life. Physically, socially and intellectually stimulating trips were more highly rated than clubbing/hedonistic or less active trips. Both short and long holidays were significant with winter breaks considered by nearly half the respondents to be the most beneficial. A short break of one to three nights was considered likely to generate benefits which lasted on average for a month after the trip. Longer holidays (seven nights or more) on average generated benefits lasting slightly longer than two months (66 days). Whilst helpful in providing a general pattern of holiday-taking benefits, this study reflected upon the holiday-taking population in general. The needs of specific groups, young people for instance, were not considered. To investigate this an empirical study was conducted which focused upon determining the perceptions of young people undergoing treatment for cancer towards the contribution of holiday-taking to health and wellbeing.

Methods

A total of twenty-five informants contributed to this study: eight cancer patients aged sixteen to nineteen (see **Table 1**); four health professionals (one social worker, one play specialist and two paediatric oncology nurses); eleven family members (eight parents, one brother and two grandparents); and two friends (aged fifteen and seventeen). Informants were accessed through the YOU at Christie Hospital, National Health Service (NHS) Trust, Manchester, UK.

A wide range of cancer forms were represented including brain, spinal, Hodgkin's disease (cancer of the lymphatic system) and osteo-sarcoma (cancer of the bones, muscles and tendons). Treatment programmes undertaken consisted of varying combinations of surgery, chemotherapy and radiotherapy. Post-treatment, patients were visiting Christie Hospital on a bi-monthly, monthly, two monthly, three monthly or six monthly basis. Interviews were conducted and recorded by the researcher between January 2000 and March 2001.

Table 1   Characteristics of cancer patients

Name (altered)	Age	Primary Cancer	Employment Status Post- Diagnosis	Travel Post- Diagnosis
Cathy	18	Spinal	Education	Domestic VFR
Mark	17	Osteo-Sarcoma	Unemployed	Domestic VFR
Peter	16	Brain	Education (p/t)	None
Susan	18	Ewings-Sarcoma	Education	Domestic VFR
Karen	16	Hodgkin's	Employed	Domestic
Julie	17	Pnet tumour	Education	Domestic
Matthew	17	Brain	Unemployed	Domestic VFR
Anna	15	Brain/spinal	Education (p/t)	None

Source: Primary data.
VFR: Visiting friends and relatives

Recognising that earlier research by Mathieson (1999) and Owens and Payne (1999) had demonstrated the value of undertaking qualitative research into the field of ill-health, death and dying, techniques such as individual interviews, group interviews, oral histories and participant observation were built into the study methodology. This was supplemented by the use of telephone discussions, letters, personal accounts and health diaries. The interview schedule developed by Mathieson and Stam (1995) was adopted and adapted as it had been previously applied in a broader sense to develop cancer narratives. Approaches to conducting the interviews were discussed with the Hospital facilitators and the interview questions piloted on these services. Potential informants were encouraged to select an appropriate interview location. The majority elected to be interviewed at home, whilst the remainder within the Hospital environment.

The data were analysed via template analysis, also known as 'codebook analysis' or 'thematic coding', a technique which consists of four parts (Crabtree and Miller, 1999: p. 166):

(a) creating a code manual or coding scheme, (b) hand or computer coding the text, (c) sorting segments to get all similar text in one place, and (d) reading the segments and making the connections that are subsequently corroborated and legitimized.

Reference to related research, particularly the ETC study (ETC, 2000) helped to develop the template. The list of codes were applied and re-modified as the primary data collection and analysis progressed.

Stage One: Pre-holiday

Selection for the holiday was undertaken by the medical social worker in consultation with medical staff at the Hospital, the patient and their families. Ten holiday places were available and were filled by five female and five male participants (eight cancer patients and two friends). Personal interviews were conducted with eight of the participants and a guardian in their homes and lasted between one and two hours. Two participants were unavailable to meet in person prior to the trip but instead completed the questions in their own time and returned their responses to the researcher. The viewpoint of a guardian was also supplied in these two cases.

Stage Two: During the holiday

Informants' perceptions, experiences and emotions during the holiday were recorded individually within a 'holiday health diary'. Such an approach to qualitative data collection has been successfully used previously on a number of occasions. Miller *et al.*, (1999) for example consider the methodological scope of such a tool in the study of low back pain. It is argued that this approach encourages free and uninhibited descriptions of perceptions and experiences on a day to day basis, something which in itself may offer therapeutic benefits. In justifying the adoption of such a technique Miller *et al.*, (1999: p. 42) argue that "the diary is more reliable than retrospective recall alone and would seem to be a useful tool for therapists of all modalities".

Stage Three: Post-holiday

During the three weeks following the holiday a further interview was conducted with each of the participants and their guardians. Interviews lasted approximately one hour and again took place in the interviewee's home. Informants were asked to reflect back upon the holiday, to talk about their different experiences and to comment upon their feelings, attitudes and outlook since returning from the holiday. To assist recall reference was made to their 'holiday health diary'. Additional to this, long-term reflections and aspirations were also questioned.

Results and discussion

Reasons for participation in the trip proved to be many and varied. Reflecting upon the primary motives suggested (see **Table 2**) it became clear that for all the young people, the trip was seen as a distraction, an opportunity to escape from everyday life, a life governed to varying degrees by illness and meet new friends in the process. As such, the fact that the holiday was in Scotland was really of little primary significance. The trip could have been to any one of a number of destinations and it would have been likely to hold a similar attractiveness. Parallels can be drawn between these findings and comments made by the psychologist David Lewis who, reflecting upon the nature of contemporary tourism behaviour, argues "we don't go *to* places we escape *from* places. We are escaping *from* environments that we find intolerable, or boring or too routine" (quoted in Bell, 1991).

In contrast, for two members of the group, Susan and Peter, Scotland itself acted as the 'pull' factor (Dann, 1976; 1977) in their decision-making process. That said, even for these two, Scotland symbolised something quite different. For Peter the pubs and shops of Glasgow were the key attractions whilst for Susan it was the romance of Scotland which inspired her to travel. Such factors are significant as they act as a reminder of the impressionable

Table 2   Primary reasons for participation

Relaxing and getting away from everything […] being independent again […] oh and being with bald people like me.   [Cathy]
Getting away and clearing me head for the first time since being ill.   [Mark]
A chance to have a break from what we've been through in the past couple of years.   [Karen]
Having a good time and doing my own thing.   [Julie]
Lounging around and doing nothing and not feeling guilty about it for a change (Matthew) thought it would be a laugh to meet some new friends.   [Tom]
A chance to be myself for a change.   [Paul]
Learning about other people's experiences and having some fun for a change. [Anna]

Source: Primary data

nature of this age group and the fact that, aside from everything they had been through, they were still young people coping with the turbulence of adolescence.

Perceived effects of holiday-taking

Whilst travel was not without complication, indeed both psychological and physical health matters featured on many occasions as inhibiting travel participation, it is beyond the scope of this paper to report such matters here (see instead Hunter-Jones, 2004). The focus here rather is to reflect upon the perceived contribution the holiday made to everyday life.

Personal health: psychological

Without exception, all informants indicated on at least one occasion that they felt the holiday had been of benefit to their personal health. For Matthew simply the break away was significant as it distracted him from the everyday tedium he had begun to accept as a way of life. Anna spoke of being able to relax more easily which in turn had a beneficial impact upon her sleeping patterns. Mark, Peter and Tom all felt that the holiday had helped "lift their spirits" (Tom) making them feel much "calmer" (Mark) and "healthier" (Peter and Mark). Whilst to Cathy, not being at odds with everyone around her for once proved significant.

Alongside direct references such as this, improved health status was demonstrated through a range of indirect statements including:

"Felt like I could have a laugh and cope with things." [*Peter*]

"I learnt a lot from Cathy about how to feel better in myself." [*Anna*]

"It was great being part of a group ... felt really part of something which made me feel happy." [Susan]

"Liked the activities ... helped keep me in shape." [*Julie*]

Such findings link closely with the ETC's (2000) observations that holidays may be beneficial to health in terms of physical relaxation, stress relief, emotional and physical wellbeing, relationships and social inclusion.

Personal health: physical

Three informants, Karen, Cathy and Anna made reference to how the holiday had physically helped them. For Karen coping with the dual demands of illness and employment had, she suggested "made me feel really shattered" (Karen). Agreeing to take part in the trip Karen hoped to "have a laugh, oh and a rest from work!". For Cathy and Anna the physical effects were more tangible. Both were coping with the demands of impaired mobility. Both acknowledged pre-trip the importance of trying to exercise, walk and seeing a physiotherapist regularly. Both had also lost enthusiasm to do so. Cathy was angry as she had been told that her walking would be impaired long-term. Rather than being directly related to the treatment she received, Cathy blamed her condition on her GP for failing to make a correct diagnosis early enough. Anna, in contrast, the most recently treated in the group was more despondent than angry finding it difficult to believe that her walking would ever improve again. Yet post-trip it was apparent, both visually and through an attitude change, that mobility in both cases had been enhanced. The reasons for such were twofold. First:

"...being with the others sort of brought you out of yourself and made you stop thinking of yourself all the time and have the confidence to try things for yourself ... you didn't want to be left out so you tried harder to walk I suppose." [*Cathy*]

Second, it was supported by the swimming opportunity they were provided with during the trip. Both Cathy and Anna spoke independently of their enjoyment of swimming prior to illness. Both had stopped swimming as a result of treatment, both because of being self-conscious about surgical scars. Yet both also recognised that swimming was a desirable activity for them to participate in to help improve their impaired mobility. The swimming in Scotland took place in a privately hired pool. During the post-trip interview Anna commented upon the significance of this:

> "I thought that were really good just us having the pool to ourselves it really helps you get back your confidence when you're with people in the same position ... you feel better about doing things when you're at home too."

Social effectiveness

Relationships with friends for most informants had altered in some way since the original diagnosis. Peter spoke of no longer being able to participate in sports events with friends as he had pre-illness. Cathy and Anna were both frustrated at how difficult it was for them to "meet up with friends" (Anna) and to "go shopping and out at night" (Cathy). Whilst for Matthew the shock of how little support his friends had been able to provide him with, he described as "probably one of the hardest parts of trying to deal with things". Such a predicament is not uncommon and may represent one of the most isolating features of cancer at this age.

Conversations with all the informants post-Scotland confirmed that with the exception of only one, the remainder all felt that they had established new friendships as a result of the holiday. Contact details had been exchanged and contact made, group members referring to the use of mobile phones "to text each other" (Karen and Paul) and the internet using e-mail as their preferred media for keeping in touch with each other. Effectively technology in this context represents one of the "tools" Jackson *et al.*, (1993) referred to as providing a means for the individual to "negotiate" their way through obstacles to leisure participation. Separate conversations with Karen and Susan, Peter and Julie also reflected upon just how important it was to be aware of others in a similar situation:

> "Susan, Julie and I were all admitted to Christie the same time, our [code] numbers followed each other .... To be honest we got to know

each other really well ...]it was a great help knowing you weren't alone and that others understood what you were going through." [*Karen*]

Self-image

Conversations with four members of the group, Cathy, Anna, Susan and Karen, pre-trip, when talking about problems they had faced due to illness focused in each case pointedly upon the problems of hair loss through treatment. Karen's remarks summarised the general feeling:

"It's weird really, you don't think about it [i.e. hair loss] until it's not there and then you can't seem to get away from people with long hair ... it just really gets to you ... you feel like everyone's looking at you, staring as if they know." [*Karen*]

Interestingly enough no male informants raised the matter at all. Yet even given the gender gap the significance of such conversations should not be underestimated for as Ratcliffe (1999) discussing the concept of body image argues "how patients perceive their physical appearance can have a positive or negative affect on their level of anxiety/depression". Indeed singling out the devastation caused through hair loss alone, Ratcliffe (1999) suggests that to many, such loss leads to heightened insecurity, isolation and loss of sexuality and has the potential to reduce empowerment and diminish self-identity. Reflecting post-trip upon which moments she found most satisfying, the Social Worker returned to the issue of hair loss remarking:

"When I saw Anna sitting with the group, laughing away and swinging her wig around, yes I think that was a really important moment ... for her to do that, well, she must have felt really comfortable."

As did Susan:

"I just felt really comfortable ... we all had short hair and it didn't feel like a problem or big deal at all. It's hard to explain really but it just felt great and made you think "so what?" for once."

Regaining independence

Conversations with a number of informants demonstrated that the holiday acted as a conduit transferring dependency from family to new friends. Susan spoke in an animated fashion about the fun she had had pre-trip planning the holiday with a friend. Whilst Peter, Mark, Karen and Matthew each felt that they had regained some independence through the sheer realisation that it was possible to survive and get on with everyday life even after the experience of secondary cancer. For one group member time spent together with others in a similar situation itself had a particularly significant impact. During conversations with Cathy post-holiday, the researcher observed a heightened awareness within the informant of the needs and emotions of others than had been evident in the pre-trip interview. Referring to a friendship which had developed between herself and another group member who was experiencing similar health issues, Cathy commented "It was great sharing a room with Anna. I'd had so long of everyone looking after me it just felt really nice to be able to think about her and not just myself for a change". The holiday had enabled Cathy to see past her own cir-cumstances and allowed her to regain lost independence through helping others, help which Anna on numerous occasions commented she drew strength from.

A significant 'emotional' beneficiary of the holiday proved to be those in the caring role. The role of principal carer or emotional support where 'children' with cancer are concerned was found by Faulkner et al., (1995: p. 68) most commonly to be the mother. Reviewing the complexities of the caring role these researchers pointed out:

> "Four mothers ... had to give up work to look after their ill child ... wanted to do this, the loss of income incurred at a time when there were many additional costs was a major concern ... . Several mentioned the social isolation they experienced."

A number of the mothers confirmed that they had been with their 'child' for twenty four hours a day, seven days a week since their diagnosis. A number had totally altered their daily routines leaving work and other social activities. Given this commitment it is not surprising that each expressed specific concerns about letting their 'child' participate in the Scotland holiday. The comments of one parent whose son was part of the group summarised many of the reasons commonly expressed: "Well I figured it would be a great break for him away from his nagging mum [laughs] and younger brother". She had herself given up work at the time of diagnosis to become fully involved in the caring role. A number of parents spoke of their feelings of guilt attached to letting their 'child' go to Scotland. Another mother who had not left her "child's" side since the original diagnosis was adamant to point out what the holiday was not about: "It's not about giving mum and dad a break … . I'd hate it if I thought that's why she thought I'd agreed to her going". Such a concern was voiced by a number of other guardians also. Interestingly enough conversations with the participants with the exception of one case, did not even touch upon such concerns.

Future career prospects

Whilst most group members showed little concern about future career aspirations two were acutely conscious of the obstacles poor health had created for them. Conversing with Cathy pre-trip it became clear the extent to which poor health had affected her. She was anxious, concerned and held out little hope of being able to progress in the areas she had, pre-illness, hoped to. Similarly, conversing with Mark pre-trip the researcher observed a tension on the subject of his employment prospects:

> "I used to work at the garage up the road before all this happened [reference to leg amputation]. He [the garage owner] says he'll take me back, but it's all held up 'coz of health and safety things … he reckons he can sort it but it's taking some time."

The employment and future prospects of adolescents in this situation have been the focus of a number of studies, many of which reach similar conclusions: cancer patients can and do face employment discrimination and barriers additional to those faced by the general population. Rejection from the armed services, education and problems in gaining life and health insurance were recorded by Teta *et al.*'s (1986) research, whilst job discrimination was a feature of research by Wasserman *et al.*, (1987); Fobair *et al.*, (1986) and Feldman (1980). Such barriers are not always a consequence of bureaucratic controls. Yet, in the context of this research, health and safety legislation intended to create an appropriate environment for Mark to function within had inadvertently resulted in his prolonged isolation and added to his increasing sense of despair.

Yet in direct contrast, post-trip, both informants exhibited quite different outlooks, shifting from being externally to internally controlled. Cathy had begun to make a concerted effort to move forward with her career plans again re-starting her 'A' level course and investigating what opportunities were open to her. Later conversations with Mark revealed a similar pattern. Rather than simply being despondent and resigned to thinking that complications were inevitable, he had decided to confront matters head on and investigate other options available if barriers existed. When questioned as to what had changed since the pre-trip interview Cathy commented:

> "Well I suppose it was realising that I'm not the only one going through all this [illness] ... others have before and survived and got on so really it's down to me to get myself sorted ... I mean if the nurses [and Liz] were bothered enough to take us away I should get on with things now myself."

Mark also followed a similar line of thinking:

> "You know the staff were all brilliant. Nothing was a problem for them. I suppose it just makes you realise that not everyone's got it in for you, some people really do want to help. I feel like I owe it to them to get on with it [i.e. job hunting]."

For the two informants the holiday had helped to boost both their energy and confidence levels increasing their capacity to confront many of the psychological barriers, often self-generated, that they were dealing with individually pre-trip.

Socially responsible behaviour

Eiser (1993: p. 65) suggests that "it is possible that the experience of chronic disease sets children apart from their healthy age-mates". She further argues that feelings such as aggression and loneliness can influence social competence and reflect mild behavioural problems which may act as both intrinsic and extrinsic barriers to social adjustment. One behavioural consequence of illness was the negative impact illness had had upon the daily routine of the individual. Attempting to set up pre-trip interviews the researcher observed that five group members were unable to meet during the morning as they did not surface until lunch time or early afternoon, then remaining awake and active until the early hours of the following morning: "What's the point of getting up early, there's nothing to do ... . It's better to get up later and wait for your mates to call round after school ... then you've got something to fill your time with" (Peter). Of the three informants who did not conform to this pattern, two were in full-time education (Susan and Julie) and one (Karen), in full-time employment, the structured day, each suggested, providing a much needed routine.

In contrast, setting up interviews post-trip the researcher observed a very different pattern emerging. None of the informants were uncomfortable with a morning meeting; instead where timing complications arose it was in each case related to the fact that the informant was active doing other things, not a situation which had been evident previously. When questioned as to what had changed since the pre-trip conversations Cathy summed up much of the group sentiment:

> "Well I suppose I've got more energy now I mean I feel like I can do things again ... yeh, I just felt really fed up all the time before so now I've got on with other things as well like picking up my 'A' level course again, oh and I can even get up in the morning again now (laughs). I thought it was because of the illness I couldn't but now I realise that I was just dead bored."

Conclusions

This paper has concentrated upon investigating the relationship between ill-health, adolescence and holiday-taking. A holiday to Scotland has provided the focus for this investigation with a number of key issues emerging.

First, when presented with the opportunity to travel to Scotland all the young people agreed to do so with a wide range of motives cited including travelling to "have a good time" or to "relax". Such motivators are by no means unique to this study and they correlate closely with the findings of a considerable number of motivational papers including for instance the work of Krippendorf (1987) and Dann (1976; 1977). They may be relevant to any age group or indeed any combination of travel characteristics be it domestic or international travel.Second, being part of a group who had shared in differing ways the experience of illness was considered to be important. It was suggested to put each at their ease, generating feelings of happiness and understanding (affiliation). It also helped to facilitate group cohesion and contributed to the socialisation process necessary during adolescence. In particular the fact that the holiday was *organised* and was organised *through Christie Hospital* was significant as it provided the necessary encouragement to travel, so often lacking for many of the group members, and also offered an essential support, particularly in the form of those 'staffing' the holiday, for those in a caring role.

Most significantly though whilst each member viewed the holiday in different ways, all perceived the trip to play an important role in returning them to a pattern of "normal" everyday life. As such the perceived effects identified extended beyond simply the holiday environment and impacted upon general wellbeing contributing in varying ways to: personal health;

social effectiveness; personal identity; self-image; regaining independence; future career aspirations; and socially responsible behaviour. One particularly extensive study which encapsulates many of these themes was a seven year study undertaken by Hendry et al., (1993). Investigating the relationship between adolescence, lifestyle and issues of sport, drugs, school, friendship, health and peer group pressure, this research questioned the role that leisure plays in young people's lives. Ultimately leisure was shown to play a significant role in facilitating the transitional process of adolescence so much so that to exclude or restrict such involvement it was argued is likely to have long-term implications for the healthy development of an individual.

Comparing the perceived effects of holiday-taking determined in this study with Hendry's et al. (1993) findings (see **Table 3**) suggests that, even where health is impaired, holiday-taking may also play a far more significant role today in underpinning the transitional process of adolescence than the activity has been credited with thus far.

Table 3   *The contribution of holiday-taking to adolescent development*

The Personal and Social Learning Tasks of Adolescence (Hendry *et al.*, 1993: p. 8)	Primary data (see results and discussion)
Achieving new and more mature relations with the age mates of both sexes	Social Effectiveness
Achieving a masculine or feminine social role	Self-Image
Accepting one's physique and using the body effectively	Self-Image
Achieving emotional independence of parents	Regaining Independence
Preparing for marriage and family life	Social Effectiveness
Preparing for an economic career	Future Career Prospects
Acquiring a set of values and an ethical system as a guide to behaviour: developing an ideology	Socially Responsible Behaviour
Desiring and achieving socially responsible behaviour	Socially Responsible Behaviour

Acknowledgements

The author would like to acknowledge and thank the staff, patients and their families linked with the YOU, Christie Hospital NHS Trust, Manchester, UK, who participated in this research. She would also like to acknowledge and thank her research supervisors Professor Howard Hughes (Manchester Metropolitan University, UK) and Professor Stephen Clift (Canterbury and Christ Church College, Canterbury, UK) for their support and guidance.

References

Bell, N. (1991) 'Wish you weren't here!', BBC Production in Association with The Discovery *Channel. First* shown 25th January. Bristol: BBC Bristol.

Coleman, J. C. and Hendry, L. B. (1990) *The nature of adolescence* (2nd Edn). London: Routledge.

Crabtree, BF. and Miller, WL. (eds) (1999) *Doing qualitative research*(2nd Edn). London: Sage Publications, pp. 163–177.

Dann, G. (1976) 'The holiday was simply fantastic', *The Tourist Review* Vol. 31, No. 3: pp. 19–23.

———— (1977) 'Anomie, ego-enhancement and tourism', *Annals of Tourism Research* 4: pp. 184–194.

Eiser, C. (1993) *Growing up with a chronic disease. The impact on children and their families*. London: Jessica Kingsley Publishers Ltd.

English Tourism Council (ETC) (2000) *Holiday benefits – Topline results*. ETC Research and Intelligence. February.

Family Holiday Association (1993) *Omnimed survey*. Surrey: Taylor Nelson Healthcare (unpublished).

———— (1996) 'Families feel the benefit of a breath of fresh air', *BMA Review* 13 March.

Faulkner, A. Peace, G. and O'Keefe, C. (1995) *When a child has cancer*. London: Chapman and Hall.

Feldman, F. C. (1980) *Work and cancer health histories: Work expectations and experiences of youth with cancer histories (ages 13–23)*. Oakland California: America Cancer Society.

Fobair, P. Hoppe, R. T. Bloom, J. Cox, R. Varghese, A and Spiegel, D. (1986) 'Psychosocial problems among survivors of hodgkin's disease', *Journal of Clinical Oncology.* 4: pp. 805–814.

Hendry, L. B. Shucksmith, J. Love, J. G. and Glendinning, A. (1993) *Young people's leisure and lifestyles*. London: Routledge.

Hunter-Jones, P. (2004) 'Young people, holiday-taking and cancer — An exploratory study', *Tourism Management* Vol 25, No. 2: pp. 249–258.

Jackson, E. L. Crawford, D. W. and Godbey, G. (1993) 'Negotiation of leisure constraints', *Leisure Sciences* 15: pp. 1–11.

Krippendorf, J. (1987) *Understanding the holidaymakers. The impact of leisure and tourism*. Oxford: Heinemann.

Mathieson, C. M. (1999) Interviewing the ill and the healthy in Murray, M. and Chamberlain, K. (eds) (1999) *Qualitative health psychology. Theories and methods*. London: Sage Publications, pp. 117–132.

Mathieson, C. and Stam, H. J. (1995) 'Renegotiating identity: cancer narratives', *Sociology of Health and Illness*, 17, 283–306 in Murray, M. and Chamberlain, K. (eds) (1999) *Qualitative health psychology. Theories and methods*. London: Sage Publications, pp. 117–132.

Miller, J. S. Stanley, I. M. and Pinnington, M. A. (1999) 'The health diary: A window into the low back pain experience', in Senior, P. (ed) (1999) *Culture, health and the arts world symposium. Symposium Abstracts, Manchester Metropolitan University*. Macclesfield: Complete Congress Services Limited.

Owens, R. G. and Payne, S. (1999) 'Qualitative research in the field of death and dying', in Murray, M. and Chamberlain, K. (eds) (1999) *Qualitative health psychology. Theories and methods*. London: Sage Publications, pp. 148–163.

Ratcliffe, P. (1999) 'Headstart: Improving body image of women cancer patients', Paper presented to Culture, Health and the Arts Conference, April, Manchester: Manchester Metropolitan University.

Teta, M. J., Del Po, M. C., Kasl, S. V., Meigs, J. W., Myers, M. H. and Mulvihill, J. J. (1986) 'Psychosocial consequences of childhood and adolescent cancer survival', *Journal of Chronic Disease* 39: pp. 751–759.

Wasserman, A. L. Thompson, E. L. Wilimas, J. A. and Fairclough, J. (1987) 'The psychological status of survivors of childhood/adolescent hodgkin's disease', *Archives of Disease in Childhood* 141: pp. 636–641.

THE FAMILY EXPERIENCE OF NATURE

Margot Edwards and Kaye Thorn
Massey University, Auckland, New Zealand

Introduction

Leisure and tourism have been identified as growth industries by world futurists. Moutinho (2000) has further suggested that there will be two key areas of growth in tourism. The first of these is an increasing awareness of the environment, and hence an increase in ecotourism and nature related tourism. The second reflects a desire to create more of a work-life balance, and to integrate family holidays with business travel. This study therefore explores these two trends in more detail, focusing on family perceptions of nature experiences that were purposely chosen as part of a planned holiday. Many parents believe in the statement made by New Zealand Tourism chief Wally Stone that nature triggers "experiences that can touch the soul" (Brook, 2002: p. A18) and thus, seek such opportunities for their children when on holiday.

Researching these kinds of experiences requires more than standard quantitative methods. The complications and complexities of human-nature experiences was highlighted by Stewart (1998) who challenged future researchers to explore leisure experiences, as they existed in various states of mind, by more innovative methods. Although this challenge has been heeded by some researchers (see for example, Schanzel and McIntosh, 2000), more research is needed to explore how participants construct stories and meanings of their experiences and how they will "embed their emergent stories in the context of their daily lives" (Borrie and Roggenbuck, 2001: p. 226).

The lack of in-depth qualitative studies into the experiential aspect of leisure and/or tourism activities, in general, have been highlighted by Lee,

Dattilo and Howard (1994), Freysinger (1994), Siegenthaler and O'Dell (2000) Hull, Stewart and Yi (1992) and Beaumont (1999). McIntyre and Roggenbuck (1998) utilised the qualitative Experience Sampling Method (ESM) to examine the nature of the nature experience as it unfolded. The ESM incorporates an analysis of respondent's personal accounts of the experience. In-depth interviewing methods have been used in leisure settings by Wearing (1990) in her study with new mothers and their access to personal leisure, and Shaw and Dawson (2001) in the area of purposive family leisure. Within the New Zealand natural context, Schanzel and McIntosh (2000) investigated the personal and emotive context of wildlife viewing of penguins through the use of in-depth interviews.

The richness of data provided in these studies generated multiple possibilities, in terms of an enhanced understanding of the relationship between the individual, family, society and the natural environment. For example, Schnazel and McIntosh (2000) identified glimmers of ecological hope when they found that five of their respondents gained an "enhanced environmental consciousness as a result of their wildlife viewing experience" (p. 47). Two further respondents, in that penguin wildlife study, thought they would become more involved in conservation work as a result of the nature interaction. It is important to recognise here, of course, that intentions do not always equate with actions (Orams, 1995).

It thus appeared, to the current authors, that the in-depth interview approach was an appropriate tool to unlock key elements of human–nature interactions and to capture the experiences of nature tourism. It was also felt that this exploration of the family and nature experience did not lend itself easily to the type of positivistic methodologies often used in tourism and leisure research, and was in part the reason for using a qualitative approach as a framework for the study. In-depth interviews with mothers and pre-teen children would allow the exploration of the process of organising such "nature" experiences. It would also elicit the families' expectations of such experiences and examine their post-trip recollections.

This paper reviews literature relating to the general area of the family holiday nature experience, derived from research from the fields of (Siegenthaler and O'Dell, 2000) leisure and the tourism. While the interviews were originally designed as the exploratory phase of a nation-wide survey, it is hoped that the voices of the participants in this current study may be used as a guide for tourism operators and policy makers to explore a wider range of management issues.

Literature review

A tourism experience does not simply happen — there must be first be an expressed desire to partake of this experience (the motivation for tourism), and there must be a plan, with corresponding decisions being made, for the experience. Tourism motivation is a popular theme in the literature (see for example, Crompton, 1979; Pearce, 1993; Kozak, 2002) and is beyond the bounds of this current study. Decision making however, is paramount to this study.

Decision-making

The decision-making process can be disaggregated into several key phases, including the initial concept, the research and planning stage, and the actual purchase of the tourism product (Ryan, 2000). Within the family, various members of the family may have different roles (Kolter *et al.*, 1999). Several authors (see for example, Fodness, 1992; Wang *et al.*, 2004) have focused on the role of parents in terms of holiday decision-making. Most of the early research focused on families headed by heterosexual couples and examined the relative influence of females and males as purchasers (see Shaw, 1997). Three types of decision-making combinations have been reported — husband-dominant, wife-dominant, and joint decision making (Fodness, 1992). Most holiday decisions tend to be joint ones, although women tend to take the dominant role in the research and planning stage. Bialeschki and Pearce (1995) who focused on lesbian families, also found that the decision-making was largely joint.

Child's influence

Other studies acknowledge the influence of children in the decision-making process (Thornton *et al.*, 1997, Seaton and Tagg, 1995). The research shows that children have a limited influence in holiday decision-making, although the child's needs and preferences may be accommodated by the parents (Nichols and Snepenger, 1999). Shaw (1997 p. 51), refers to a "choice-obligation dichotomy" in family decision making. An example of this occurs between the child's obligation to participate, when the parents organise and pay for a four-day wilderness tramp, and the child's willingness to experience the novel and fun aspects that occur along the way. This dichotomy, acknowledged as 'choice versus constraint' by Larson, Gillman and Richards (1997: p. 81) was illustrated in their findings that during a family outing, the father reported "great enjoyment", the mother reported "stress" and the daughter reported "boredom".

Such variance in perceptions is inherent in experiences of family leisure as perceived by adolescents and highlights the likelihood of family members who feel obligated to participate experiencing less satisfaction or lower perceived leisure freedom. Shaw's earlier research (1992a, 1992b) had urged an exploration of such negative and positive factors on the diversity within family's skills and interests.

Although little attention has been given to the child's role in the holiday decision-making process, several authors have examined the child's role in the choice of recreational activities in a family context (see for example, Howard and Madrigal, 1990). Szybillo and Sosaine (1977) further noted the importance of a child's influence on minor decisions while on holiday, in choosing the restaurant for dinner, or going on a family trip. Wang *et al.,* (2004) specifically examine the role of the parents and the child in group package tour choice, finding that wives are dominant in the information search stage, with both parents involved in the key decision making. The child's influence was fairly limited in this situation.

Seaton and Tagg (1995) conducted surveys of 2824 school children in four European nations to explore the perceived role of children in vacation decisions. Three conclusions from this large multinational study are relevant to the context of this current paper. Firstly, the majority of children surveyed played some part in the holiday decisions-making process and, secondly, the children viewed the decision making as syncratic (both parents involved), although mothers were seen as the final decision makers. Finally, the involvement of the children in the decision making resulted increased the possibility of an optimum outcome for the family group as a whole, while not doing so increased the chances of an unhappy child on holiday.

Nature experiences

Although many families seek the restorative effects of nature experiences whilst on holiday (Hartig *et al.,* 1991), there appears to be a lack of empirical evidence that links the activity with specific benefits. These authors suggest that the most elusive component of a holiday or a leisure activity, is the experience itself. Furthermore, very little data exists which addresses "the attitudes and reactions of children to family activities, nor of the outcomes, beneficial or otherwise, for these family members" (Shaw, 1997, p. 109).

Positive psychological effects

Suggestions that leisure experiences that occur while on holiday have a beneficial effect on an individual's psyche are prevalent in the tourism and leisure literature. One empirical study that provides a concept, relevant to this current study, is Hartig *et al.*, (1991), who suggested that natural settings, including urban parks and wilderness areas, may facilitate recovery from the "mental fatigue induced by the demands of modern life" (p. 24). Their findings also raise the possibility that people, if exposed to therapeutic environments, could be inoculated against the pressures of life. It may be that laughing and having fun are important components in family nature experiences and may be sought by families who lead very busy life styles. Ryan (1994) provided powerful evidence that mental relaxation was the highest motivating factor for British holiday-makers, although he could not link the emergence of more active life styles to changes in his participants motivations.

Csikszentmihalyi and Larsen (1984) found that experiences during leisure were the most positive experiences among adolescents and Shaw, Kleiber and Caldwell (1995) noted the positive link between identity formation and certain types of activities and concluded that physical leisure activities, which encouraged independence and autonomy, were developmentally beneficial for adolescent females.

Psychological motivations for recreational activities, such as penguin peering or wild water kayaking, are directly addressed in a review by Mannell and Iso-Ahola (1987) following from the work by Iso-Ahola (1984, 1982) which developed a model explicating motivational dimensions of leisure, in terms of seeking and escaping. Iso-Ahola's theory highlights the importance of two psychological benefits of recreational travel stem from the interaction between two forces: escaping from routine and/or stressful environments and the desire for recreational opportunities. These two forces are further moderated by personal or interpersonal dimensions which appear to be changing as society evolves, for example, there has been an increase in the choice of 'escape' type destinations, as people seek refuge from highly-stimulating lives, and this is linked to a trend towards more frequent but shorter vacations (Mannell and Iso-Ahola, 1987).

Escapism, therefore, may be a key consideration in the decision to include nature experiences as an integral part of a family holiday. The increasing likelihood that tourists will search for "the pristine, the primitive, the natural, that which is as yet untouched by modernity" (Cohen, 1988, p. 374) has been highlighted by anthropologists but the extent to which peoples lives are changed as a result of this encounter is as yet unanswered. Stronza (2001) argues that researchers do not "know what kinds of travel heightens consciousness or educates people in particular ways ... [and] we do not know how their thoughts, feelings, or behaviours changes as a results of what they have seen in host destinations" (p. 277). Patterson, Watson, Williams and Roggenbuck (1998) sought to investigate these feelings and behaviours with in-depth interviews of recreational walkers immediately following a wilderness experience in Juniper Prairie Florida. A key finding that emerged from their analysis was that the theme of 'challenge' emerged in every participant's response and yet the meaning of 'challenge' was varied and complex and dependent on the participant's experience, skills and expectations. Other key themes that emerged were closeness to nature, decisions not faced in everyday environments, and stories of nature.

It may be that many parents plan holidays for the exact purpose of providing challenging or extraordinary outdoor experiences. This was shown by Hollender (1977) who provided an insight into motivations of parents who took their children on a camping holiday. It appears that a wide range of factors, such as teaching children about the outdoors, seeking the emotional satisfaction of solitude, tranquility, and un-spoilt beauty and getting away from people, may be motivations underpinning experiences in the natural environment. It may be that such motivations also exist for parents who plan nature activities within their holiday excursion.

There is a growing belief amongst environmentalists that ecological experiences, such as walking nature trails, or watching dolphins, create an appropriate mechanism for increasing ecological awareness and actions (Grob, 1995, Orams, 1995). One such study reported "mental, spiritual and psychological benefits" from viewing wildlife at the Penguin Palace on the Otago Penninsula (Schnazel and McIntosh, 2000). Several respondents in this study reported that they gained the "experience of contributing to conservation" while two respondents singled out the benefits that children gained their increased insight onto the life of penguins, for example "how they need to be protected" (Schnazel and McIntosh, 2000, p. 47). More importantly, in psychological terms, the beneficial experiences that occurred at the Penguin Palace were found to be affective and cognitive, which may be important in terms of environmental preservation.

The literature on leisure and tourism therefore provides some insight into the process of decision making about nature experiences. It is however cursory, and tells us little about the direct objectives for the experience. It has tended to examine the experience in isolation, without linking the various phases of decision making. We might know how many people are tramping in national parks, or the ages of the people, but there is a scarcity of in-depth accounts of the expectations, the actual experience and reflections about the family nature activity.

Method

Ten families (mothers and their children) were interviewed in a semi-structured manner. Eight interviews occurred in the participant homes, following the recommendations of those familiar with interviewing children (Wilson and Powell, 2001, Darlington and Scott, 2002) and two occurred at the researchers' workplace. The researchers conducted the interviews as a pair; with one taking primary responsibility for taking notes and planning additional questions, which arose from participant responses, while the other took the lead role in asking the broad pre-planned questions. The interview covered a range of questions about the family holiday experience, ranging from the process of holiday selection to the post-holiday reflections. Children were included in the interview and were encouraged to contribute to the discussions at any time. Questions, in general, were addressed to the whole group with two exceptions; the questions on holiday planning, were directed more towards the mother in order to put the children at ease and questions regarding the actual nature experience were directed towards the children in order to elicit their perceptions before their parents views were aired. The researchers aimed to overcome the parental bias highlighted by Hood, Kelley and Mayall (1996) whereby children's views, in this type of family interview situation, were overpowered by adult exchanges during the interview process. The researchers made a conscious effort to capture ideas expressed by the children and noted the frequency with which children and mothers prompted each other to recall certain events. The interviews ranged in length from one to two hours.

The families were recruited through an advertisement in a family oriented magazine that featured a lead article on family travel. Once contact had been established the participants were vetted to ensure they met the requirements for participants, having recently taken a family holiday involving at least four nights or longer and had taken their child/children under the age of twelve. They were then emailed an information letter detailing the purpose of the study, data collection and use, and their rights as participants. Participants then phoned the researchers to organise a time and place for the interview to occur.

The initial response to the advertisement was small and it became necessary to adopt a snow-ball technique to increase the sample size. Participants, immediately following the interview, were asked if they knew of anyone who had travelled with children and included a 'nature' component to the holiday. If they replied positively they were asked to email a copy of the information sheet on to any families that they thought might fit the target group.

The magazine advertisement enabled access to a group of people who were interested in family nature experiences and positively motivated towards child-inclusive-research, however, the inclusion of snow-balling meant the sample was homogeneous and thus the participants cannot be considered to be representative of the entire population.

All participants lived in the greater Auckland area of New Zealand and were from two-parent, heterosexual, above-average income families. In addition the families were of European or Pakeha descent. In all the families the father was the major income earner. Two of the mothers were in full-time paid employment outside the home, four were employed part-time and the remainder worked at home in an unpaid capacity. Such a homogeneous sample was never purposefully sought but arose coincidentally as participants responded to advertisements and as additional participants were sought through snow-ball sampling.

The sample included thirteen children, ranging in age from 5 to 12 years. Eight families had two children, and two had one child.

The analysis of the interview data was achieved using an inductive process based on qualitative techniques used in grounded theory (Strauss and Corbin, 1990, Strauss and Corbin, 1994). During the research, coding and analysis began as soon as the first interview data were collected and named. These named categories were positive codings because they were to be used directly in creating trees upon which corresponding branches, and detailed factors, could be placed. Thus our analysis identified and aggregated areas of theoretical and empirical interest in the interview transcripts (Tolich and Davidson, 1999). As experiences or perceptions were recorded as factors, they were coded and compared with new and previous factors, and consequently assigned to an existing or new category. Modification of existing categories was frequently undertaken and this was once again an ongoing reflexive process.

The initial coding process fractured the data (Strauss & Corbin, 1990) and allowed the identification of tentative categories and factors of theoretical significance. As the research progressed, the linkages between the trees, branches and factors were identified, modified, reconfirmed or removed. Through rigorous consideration of their placement a pattern emerged whereby categories became settled and additions of new factors were less frequent.

Axial coding followed the initial phase and this process helped define the categories and make connections between categories, branches and factors. The resultant Factor Trees are shown in the results and discussion section.

There were a number of specific research limitations which became apparent as the family experience of nature tourism study progressed. The first of these was the extremely homogeneous population that arose from a specific group of people who volunteered to participate in the family interview. Those families that did respond positively were, without exception, financially secure, European or Pakeha families whose main income earner was classed as a professional. In addition all of the families comprised heterosexual couples with at least one child in the pre-teen age bracket. This type of limited sampling has been criticized by Shaw (1997) who urged researchers to look beyond middle-class, two parent families. In terms of this current study, the mothers' choice of nature experience was, at times, shaped by financial considerations and the importance of this constraint is likely to be more apparent in the general population. It is expected that the nation-wide survey which will follow this initial exploration will counter this limitation.

Findings and discussion

Data collected during the study developed three core categories which were named as: nature experience choice, Mother's nature experience expectations, and post-holiday reflections. For each core category, a variety of factors were identified as having an influence on that key category. Each of these shall be discussed.

Figure 1 shows the factor tree for the first category — the choice of the nature experience. The first branch of this tree identifies the main objectives for the nature experience — what the mother wished to achieve from undertaking this trip. Almost all mothers identified the desire to have increased family time as an important variable in deciding to take the trip.

They were looking for a destination which would enable them to spend time as a family, the specific destination was not as important as the opportunity afforded by the location to spend time together. This was illustrated by Beth's comment — "There was no TV and every night we were able to sit around the fire together".

A second factor identified in the interviews, and reinforcing the findings of Cohen (1979) and Stronza (2001) was the concept of escapism, with the natural environment providing a different atmosphere and an opportunity to be away from day-to-day routines. The interviewees had specifically sought natural destinations to distance themselves from their usual lives. One

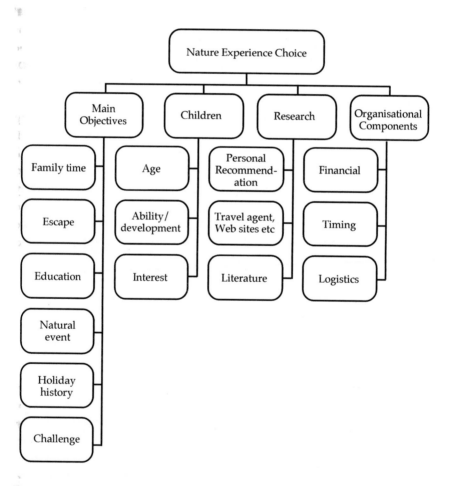

Figure 1   Factors influencing the choice of nature experience

respondent commented that their lives are so busy, and that they are on call for work at all hours, and so they intentionally choose destinations where they can not be contacted.

Education was another component of the nature experience choice. The desire to increase the knowledge of the children in some way was definitely part of the objective of the trip. For example, Maria and her husband took their two boys into the Sahara Desert:

> "I think travel is good for their education. They know a lot about the desert and more importantly, it is learning through experience rather than reading."

Increasing environmental awareness is one of the outcomes of natural experiences reported in the literature (Schanzel and McIntosh, 2000). It was also one of the objectives sought from the nature experience. Many of the mothers wished their children to learn more about the natural environment and have an actual experience within it. The nature of the interaction ranged from camping, tramping, snorkelling through to the desert experience.

The holiday history of the mother, or her partner, had a significant bearing on the objectives of the natural experience. This could be two forms — first, the mother wanted to replicate the type of holidays she had had as a child, something she had particularly enjoyed and remembered, and she wanted to ensure her children had a similar experience. Alternatively, the mother may have been denied the type of experience she wanted as a child, and therefore felt it was important to expose her children to these types of nature experience. This was eloquently expressed by Carol when asked if she had had a nature experience as a child:

> "No, I didn't … not at all. My parents would never have done that. Whereas my husband did. He went tramping with his father and things like that. He did do it and so he has a real need to engender that in his children. For me, I didn't get to do it so for me it is exciting to do it."

The significance of historical experiences and memories of childhood holidays does not appear to be a focus of the family leisure literature. These current findings suggest this may have a profound influence on the decision making process. Every interviewee mentioned either their past experiences or lack of experiences as a determining factor in the choice or type of destination.

Within the objectives for the natural experience choice, challenge was the final component. Katherine encapsulates this concept:

"I wanted to challenge, to test myself, to prove that I could do this.
Doing the tramp with the children just added to the challenge."

While several of the interviewees mentioned wanting to challenge themselves, their perceptions of challenge varied depending on their past experiences and their expectations of the experience. This finding has consonance
with Patterson *et al.*'s (1998) interviews in natural settings in the United States.

The second branch highlights the role of the children in the determination
of the natural experience. Factors such as the age of the children, their physical
capabilities, their social development and skills and their interests all had a
bearing on the choice of destination. Carol identified some of the practical
aspects of this:

"My husband and I have done a lot of travelling, and we went to
some big countries and we spent a lot of time on public transport and
we didn't want to do that with small children ... so we went to Sri
Lanka which is a relatively small island."

And Susan acknowledged the added burden of sharing experiences with
children:

"There is an extra responsibility with a child ... ."

The third branch within this category was research. As in the literature, the
women in the family definitely had the predominant role in researching the
nature experience. The research usually consisted of talking with friends for
recommendations, taking particular heed of those who were experienced
travellers or who had travelled to specific destinations with children:

"We were at a party, the day before I gave birth to my first son, and
we met this couple and they had just come back from Vietnam with
their three children. They talked about the wonderful foods and that
was inspirational". [Interview with Carol]

Travel agents were another source of information — "Dave's Mum is a travel
agent, and she kept us up to date on which resorts were a bit tired, so we had
some insider information" (Interview with Jill). Interestingly, many of the
original ideas for travel had stemmed from more general travel literature,
biographies or from the cinema. Maria commented that her interest in
travelling to Tunisia came from watching the beautiful scenery in a movie
about the country:

"It was just amazing, and I remember thinking that I would love to go there, and then I thought, well, why don't we go?"

The women interviewed were also primarily responsible for the most of the organisational components required for the trip. It was the women who checked when the school holidays were, when the peak travel seasons were, what the climate was like at that time of year, whether the passports were current and similar details. They also spent considerable time talking to the airlines for international journeys, assessing whether frequent flyer points could be used to reduce the costs of the trip. It is important to emphasise that although the respondents came from above-average income families, most of the women were engaged in either full-time or part-time employment outside the home.

Decisions about financial aspects of the planned experience were, however, more likely to be considered jointly, or, in one case, were determined by the husband. Jill was very clear that any financial decisions were her husband's:

"I should also add that if I had suggested a trip like this and Dave had said no we don't have enough money, we wouldn't have gone. He is definitely the boss with finances and he would make that call."

This latter finding differs from the literature. Fodness (1992), Wang *et al.* (2004) and Shaw (1997) all found that the financial decisions were most likely to be joint ones. However, in this instance, the husband was the sole income earner in the family, and this is likely to have an impact on financial decision making.

The second category incorporated those factors which made up the mothers' expectations of the nature experience, and this is shown in Figure 2. They had by this stage selected the type of nature experience they were going to undertake, and the specific destination. They were developing expectations of what the trip was going to be like. The expectations were similar irrespective of whether the trip was to be within New Zealand (domestic) or international. Both education and physical challenge were identified as being part of the expectations. Education focused both on the parent themselves and the child:

"It was somewhere I hadn't been but always wanted to, and I was keen for Sam to learn more about that part of the country". [Interview with Katherine]

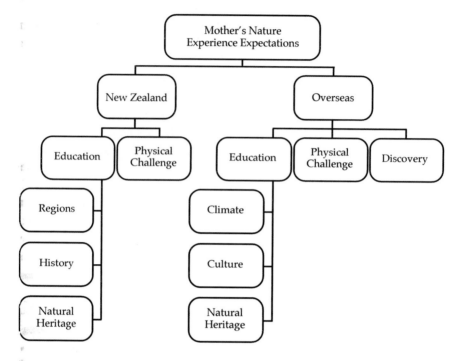

Figure 2   Factor tree of the mother's expectations of the nature experience

Within a domestic setting, the education involved learning more about a part of the country, the history and geography of that area. On an international trip, there was an expectation that the education would also involve learning about the climate and culture of the country. In many instances, there was preparation for learning — the mothers included the children in the research of the area, so the learning began before the nature experience. It is not surprising that there was also an expectation to gain an insight into the native plants and animals of the area, and a desire to experience different natural habitats and environments.

Challenge has already been identified as one of the main objectives for planning a nature experience with a family. It is interesting that challenge is still one of the expectations of the planned trip, but one that is perhaps looked on with some trepidation:

"We were a bit concerned about one day because the walk was 18.5km, and it looked really difficult." [Interview with Susan]

Those people who went overseas for their nature experience also had an expectation of discovery. While closely related to education, it is categorised separately here since it is more intangible that learning about an aspect of a country. Maria sums it up succinctly:

"I was a born traveller — when I read about these places, I have a spacious feeling come over me … this feeling of I have to go there … it was like this exotic life out there waiting for me to find … ."

The children were asked about their expectations of the nature experience that had been planned, but had little to say. John was asked specifically what his expectations were of a four day tramp and he replied that he was just "keen to give it a go". The lack of expectations of the children quite clearly reflects their age and their lack of history from which to build expectations. Shaw (1997) suggests that the literature does not examine the attitudes of children towards family activities, and this absence of preformed ideas may be one of the reasons researchers have had difficulty collecting data in this field.

The final category related to the post-experience reflections of both the mother and the child, was divided into highlights and lowlights as illustrated in Figure 3. The literature does not fully investigate the post-experience reflections of families, perhaps due to the difficulties of following up with people after their trip. The exception is perhaps Patterson *et al.*, (1998) who sought immediate response after a day spent with nature, rather than allowing for a more in-depth reflection of the experience some time later. This research specifically asked the mothers and the children to think back over their experience, and to identify both the positives and the negatives of their trip.

The mothers' highlights related directly back to the objectives she had for the nature experience. The mothers' perceptions of their achievement included coping with the unknown, achieving the physical challenge, and discovering a "can do" attitude. Carol sums this up, reflecting on a three day tramp with two young children:

"The highlights were just making it. You know it is a challenge to make it with a child. With Josh it was certainly a challenge!"

A second highlight for the mothers was family growth. This included spending time with the family, coping with adversity as a family, meeting other families with children and watching the strengthening familial bonds between the partner and child.

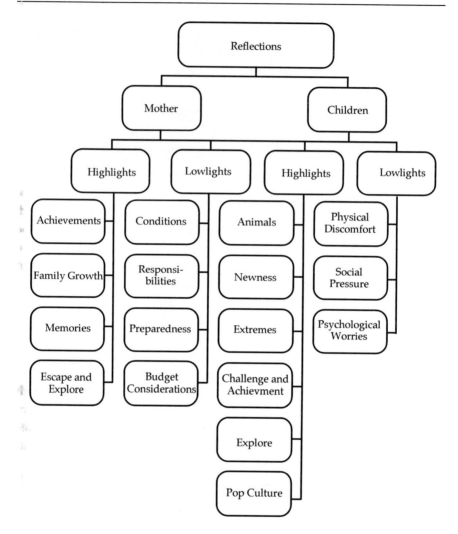

Figure 3   Reflections about the family nature experience

Memories were also an important component of the mothers' experiences. Reminiscing about past experiences or visiting previous trip destinations were part of this, as was adding new memories to their "bank" of family and nature experiences.

The final highlight identified by the mothers was the opportunity the experience provided for escaping from their daily routines and exploring a different environment. Maria's experience in the Sahara Desert strongly reflects this concept:

"I really loved the absence. The absence of bush and sea and stimulation. It was also an absence of clutter, of gear, of technology, it was just such a change. It was a nature experience that was the antitheses of everything I had ever experienced in nature, in fact there was so little sensation that for the first time in my whole life I was outside and I could hear my own heart beat because there was no noise — a total absence of sound. I was desolate when the trip ended."

The mothers' lowlights recognised the difficulties of the nature experience they had undertaken. Lack of washing facilities, being physically exhausted, being demoralised by their physical ability and struggling with extreme weather reflected the conditions that they experienced. There were also worries about the extra responsibilities they had with the children away from their usual environment, and concerns about not being prepared:

"Sri Lanka, when we got there we were a little worried. You can't plan for anything in that country … it's just this place where just about everything goes wrong and you think "what am I going to do now?" and you've just got to cope with everything" (Interview with Carol).

A final reflection of the mothers relates to budget considerations. Almost all women raised the issue of the costs of the trips they had undertaken, whether within New Zealand or overseas. However, they had also, in their reflections, weighed up these costs with the benefits obtained from the trip, and concluded that it was money well spent.

The children's highlights were more tangible than the mothers, with almost all of them enjoying an interlude with an animal of some sort.

"The highlight was the turtles and the stingray when we were snorkling." [Anna, age 8]
"And what I liked was catching eels." [Andrew, age 11]
"The camels — the hump, and the long eyelashes and their smoochy eyes — we gave them all names." [James, age 12]

The opportunity to interact with an animal that was outside their usual experience for the children remained a strong memory in their minds.

The children also enjoyed the opportunity to experience new situations and environments. They liked learning new things about nature, and the whole concept of exploring and not knowing what they were going to find. They, like their mothers, also enjoyed facing the challenge of the adventure and achieving it. John's comment, when asked how he felt about finishing a four day tramp, reflects this:

> "It was a real achievement, but I felt more relieved than anything. I was quite tired, but I had done it."

The children also identified the extremes they had experienced as highlights. This was extremes of terrain, as in the desert, or extremes of weather, being faced with flash flooding.

An interesting highlight from the children was relating their natural experience back to aspects of their everyday culture. For example, one family had spent some time in a forest in the south of New Zealand that was used for the filming of the "Lord of the Rings" trilogy, and the thought that they were in the same place as the movie actors and the characters, made the environment particularly relevant, and special.

The lowlights identified by the children in the interviews were of both a physical and a psychological nature. The children had not enjoyed being physically uncomfortable, being wet, cold or tired, nor had they enjoyed the unpleasant interactions with wildlife such as stings from jellyfish or fire ant bites. Several of them were also worried about interacting with nature, as a result of seeing nature programmes on television. For example, Andrew's commented about a snorkelling episode in Fiji:

> "Well I didn't enjoy it as much as the others — I kept thinking about the sharks that were looming out there. I enjoyed the shallows though, and chasing the fish around."

The final concern expressed by the children was related to teenage social pressure. John had not told his friends that he had tramped as it "wasn't cool" to go tramping in your holidays. A similar sentiment was expressed by another child's mother who mused over her child taking hair gel on a four day tramp! The pressure of the urban environment seems to have been transferred to the natural environment.

Conclusion

A synthesis of ideas from our findings have been drafted into a tentative model of the decision making process for family nature experiences. These are shown in Figure 4. There is a whole range of nature experience possibilities that exist and the family must choose those which best fit with their main objectives, whether these are to escape normal routines, explore or simply to spend time together as a family. Family choice is also affected by the amount of research family members are able to complete in order to fully explore the nature experience options. Once again a large amount of variation occurs between family's approach to researching the options and attempts typically range from asking friends and family to detailed searches of web sites and other literature.

Another key element in the choice of nature experiences is the mother and / or partner's nature experience history and their recalled memories of such experiences. Mothers often wanted to do the types of activities they had done with their own family or, alternatively, they wanted their children to do the types of things that they wished they had done as children.

At this stage of the process the ideal nature experience is identified, however, a range of constraints must be negotiated before an achievable

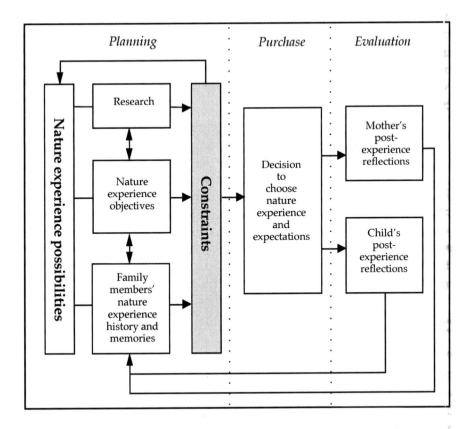

Figure 4   Proposed model of decision making for family nature experiences

nature experience is purchased. These constraints, as alluded to throughout the interviews, vary for every family and may be financial, child-specific requirements or timing details, for example, school holiday considerations. If these constraints cannot be satisfactorily overcome the family may return to reconsider the range of nature experience options.

If the family has the resources and ability to overcome the constraints, the decision to purchase now occurs and expectations about the experience are formed. These expectations are crucial elements in the process because, once the nature experience is over, the family reflect upon these, as well as their highlights and lowlights, and assess whether their expectations have or have not been met. These post-experience evaluations are then added to the rich array of histories and memories from which the family will be able to draw upon when making decisions about nature experiences in future.

References

Beaumont, N.K. (1999) *Ecotourism: The contribution of educational nature experiences to environmental knowledge, attitudes and behaviours*. Unpublished Doctor of Philosophy thesis, Griffith University, Brisbane.

Bialeschki, M. D. and Pearce, K. D. (1995) '"Who we are and what we are": The cultural construct of lesbian families', *NRPA Leisure Research Symposium*, San Antonio, TX.

Borrie, W. T. and Roggenbuck, J. W. (2001) 'The dynamic, emergent, and multi-phasic nature of on-site wilderness experiences', *Journal of Leisure Research* Vol. 33, No. 2: pp. 202–228.

Cohen, E. (1979) 'A phenomenology of tourism experiences', *Journal of Sociology* Vol. 13, No. 2: pp. 179–201.

—— (1988) 'Traditions in the qualitative sociology of tourism', *Annals of Tourism Research* Vol. 15, No. 1: pp. 29–46.

Crompton, J. (1979) 'Motivations for pleasure vacation', *Annals of Tourism Research* Vol. 6, No. 4: pp. 408–424.

Csikszentmihalyi, M. and Larson, R. (1984) *Being adolescent*. New York: Basic Books.

Darlington, Y. and Scott, D. (2002) *Qualitative research in practice: Stories from the field*. Buckingham: Allen & Unwin.

Fodness, D. (1992) 'The impact of family life cycle on the vacation decision-making process', *Journal of Travel Research* Vol. 31, No. 2: pp. 8–13.

Freysinger, V. (1994) 'Leisure with children and parental satisfaction: Further evidence of a sex difference in the experience of adult roles and leisure', *Journal of Leisure Research* Vol. 26, No. 3: pp. 212–226.

Grob, A. (1995) 'A structural model of environmental attitudes and behaviour', *Journal of Environmental Psychology* Vol. 15, No. 3: pp. 209–220.

Hartig, T., Mang, M. and Evans, G. (1991) 'Restorative effects of natural environment experiences', *Environment and Behavior* Vol. 23, No. 1: pp. 3–26.

Hollender, J. (1977) 'Motivational dimensions of the camping experience', *Journal of Leisure Research* Vol. 9, No. 2: pp. 133–141.

Hood, S., Kelley, P. and Mayall, B. (1996) 'Children as research subjects: A risky enterprise', *Children and Society* Vol. 10, No. 2: pp. 117–29.

Howard, D. R. and Madrigal, R. (1990) 'Who makes the decision — the parent or the child — the perceived influence of parents and children on the purchase of recreation services', *Journal of Leisure Research* Vol. 22, No. 3: pp. 244–258.

Hull, R. B., Stewart, W. P. and Yi, Y. K. (1992) 'Experience patterns: Capturing the dynamic nature of a recreation experience', *Journal of Leisure Research* Vol. 24, No. 3: pp. 240–252.

Iso-Ahola, S. (1982) 'Towards a social psychological theory of tourism motivation: A rejoinder', *Annals of Tourism Research* Vol. 12, No. 2: pp. 256–262.

Iso-Ahola, S. (1984) 'Social, psychological foundations of leisure and resultant implications for leisure counselling', in E. Dowd (ed) *Leisure counseling: Concepts and applications.* Charles C. Thomas, Springfield, IL, pp. 97–125.

Kolter, P., Bowen, J. and Makens, J. (1999) *Marketing for hospitality and tourism.* Upper Saddle River, N.J.: Prentice Hall International.

Kozak, M. (2002) 'Comparative analysis of tourist motivations by nationality and destinations', *Tourism Management* Vol. 23, No. 3: pp. 221–232.

Larson, R., Gillman, S. and Richards, M. (1997) 'Divergent experiences of family leisure: fathers, mothers and young adolescents', *Journal of Leisure Research* Vol. 29, No. 1: pp. 78–97.

Lee, Y., Dattilo, J. and Howard, D. (1994) 'The complex and dynamic nature of leisure experience', *Journal of Leisure Research* Vol. 26, No. 3: pp. 195–211.

Mannell, R. C. and Iso-Ahola, S. (1987) 'Psychological nature of leisure and tourism experience', *Annals of Tourism Research* Vol. 14, No. 3: pp. 314–331.

McIntyre, N. and Roggenbuck, J. (1998) 'Nature/person transactions during an outdoor adventure experience: A multi-phasic analysis', *Journal of Leisure Research* Vol. 30, No. 4: pp. 401–422.

Moutinho, L. (2000) 'Trends in tourism', in L. Moutinho (eds) *Strategic Management in tourism.* Wallingford, UK: CABI Publishing, pp. 3–16.

Nichols, C. and Snepenger, D. (1999) 'Family decision making and tourism behaviours and attitudes', in A. Pizam and T. Mansfeld (eds) *Consumer behaviour in travel and tourism.* Birmingham, NY: The Haworth Hospitality Press, pp. 135–148.

Orams, M. B. (1995) 'Towards a more desirable form of ecotourism', *Tourism Management* Vol. 16, No. 1: pp. 3–8.

Patterson, M., Watson, A., Williams, D. and Roggenbuck, J. (1998) 'An hermeneutic approach to studying the nature of wilderness experiences', *Journal of Leisure Research* Vol. 30, No. 4: pp. 423–453.

Pearce, P. L. (1993) 'Fundamentals of tourism motivation', in R. Butler (ed) *Tourism research: Critiques and challenges.* Routledge, London, pp. 113–134.

Ryan, C. (1994) 'Leisure and tourism — the application of leisure concepts to tourist behaviour — a proposed model', in R. Smith (ed) *Tourism: The state of the art.* Chichester: John Wiley, pp. 294–307.

———— (2000) 'Selecting holidays: The purchase decision and its antecedents', in S. Page (ed) *Tourism Management: Towards the new millennium.* New York: Pergamon.

Schanzel, H. A. and McIntosh, A. (2000) 'An insight into the personal and emotive context of wildlife viewing at the Penguin Place, Otago Peninsula, New Zealand.' *Journal of Sustainable Tourism* Vol. 8, No. 1: pp. 36–52.

Seaton, A. V. and Tagg, S. (1995) 'The family vacation in Europe: paedonomic aspects of choices and satisfactions', *Journal of Travel and Tourism Marketing* Vol. 4, No. 1: pp. 1–21.

Shaw, S. (1997) 'Controversies and contradictions in family leisure: An analysis of conflicting paradigms', *Journal of Leisure Research* Vol. 29, No. 1: pp. 8–112.

Shaw, S. and Dawson, D. (2001) 'Purposive leisure: Examining parental discourses on family activities', *Leisure Sciences* Vol. 23, No. 4: pp. 217–231.

Shaw, S., Kleiber, D. and Caldwell, L. (1995) 'Leisure and identify formation in male and female adolescents: A preliminary examination', *Journal of Leisure Research* Vol. 27, No. 3: pp. 245–263.

Shaw, S. M. (1992a) 'Dereifying family leisure: An examination of women's and men's everyday experiences and perceptions of family time', *Leisure Sciences* Vol. 14, No. 3: pp. 271–286.

—— (1992b) 'Research update: Family leisure and leisure services', *Parks & Recreation* Vol. 27, No. 12: pp. 13–16.

Siegenthaler, K. L. and O'Dell, I. (2000) 'Leisure attitude, leisure satisfaction, and perceived freedom in leisure within family dyads', *Leisure Sciences* Vol. 22, No. 4: pp. 281–296.

Stewart, W. P. (1998) 'Leisure as multiphase experiences: Challenging traditions', *Journal of Leisure Research* Vol. 30, No. 4: pp. 391–401.

Strauss, A. and Corbin, J. (1990) *Business of qualitative research: Grounded theory procedures and techniques*. Newbury Park, CA. : Sage.

—— (1994) 'Grounded theory methodology: An overview', in N. Denzin and Y. Lincoln (eds) *Handbook of qualitative research*. Thousand Oaks, CA: Sage, pp. 273–285.

Stronza, A. (2001) 'Anthropology of tourism: Forging new ground for ecotourism and other alternatives', *Annual Review of Anthropology* Vol. 30, No.: pp. 261–283.

Szybillo, G. and Sosanie, A. (1977) 'Family decision making: Husband, wife and children', in W. D. Perreault (ed) *Advances in Consumer Research*, 4. Association for Consumer Research, Atlanta.

Thornton, P., Shaw, G. and Williams, A. (1997) 'Tourist group holiday behaviour: The influence of children', *Tourism Management* Vol. 18, No. 5: pp. 287–297.

Tolich, M. and Davidson, C. (1999) *Starting fieldwork: An introduction to qualitative research in New Zealand*. Auckland: Oxford University Press.

Wang, K.-C., Hsieh, A.-T., Yeh, Y.-C. and Tsai, C.-W. (2004) 'Who is the decision-maker: The parents or the child in group package tours?', *Tourism Management* Vol. 25, No. 4: pp. 217–231.

Wearing, B. (1990) 'Beyond the ideology of motherhood: Leisure as resistance', *Australian and New Zealand Journal of Sociology* Vol. 26, No. 1: pp. 36–58.

Wilson, J. and Powell, M. (2001) *A guide to interviewing children: Essential skills for counsellors, social workers, police, lawyers*. New York: Routledge.

Leisure Studies Association

LSA Publications

LSA

An extensive list of publications on a wide range of leisure studies topics, produced by the Leisure Studies Association since the late 1970s, is available from LSA Publications.

Some recently published volumes are detailed on the following pages, and full information may be obtained on newer and forthcoming LSA volumes from:

LSA Publications, c/o M. McFee
email: mcfee@solutions-inc.co.uk
The Chelsea School, University of Brighton
Eastbourne BN20 7SP (UK)

Among other benefits, members of the Leisure Studies Association may purchase LSA Publications at preferential rates. Please contact LSA at the above address for information regarding membership of the Association, LSA Conferences, and LSA Newsletters.

ONLINE

Complete information about LSA Publications:

www.leisure-studies-association.info/LSAWEB/Publications.html

EVALUATING SPORT AND ACTIVE LEISURE FOR YOUNG PEOPLE

LSA Publication No. 88.   ISBN: 0 906337 99 2 [2005] pp. 236+xviii eds. Kevyn Hylton, Anne Flintoff and Jonathan Long

Contents

SPORT AND ACTIVE LEISURE YOUTH CULTURES

**LSA PUBLICATIONS NO. 86. ISBN: 0 906337 97 6 [2005] pp. 238 + xxii
eds. Jayne Caudwell and Peter Bramham**

Contents

LEISURE, SPACE AND VISUAL CULTURE: PRACTICES AND MEANINGS

LSA Publication No. 84. ISBN: 0 906337 95 X [2004] pp. 292+xxii eds. Cara Aitchison and Helen Pussard

Contents

LEISURE, MEDIA AND VISUAL CULTURE: REPRESENTATIONS AND CONTESTATIONS

**LSA Publication No. 83. ISBN: 0 906337 94 1 [2004] pp. 282
eds. Cara Aitchison and Helen Pussard**

Contents

SPORT, LEISURE AND SOCIAL INCLUSION

LSA Publication No. 82. ISBN: 0 906337 933 [2003] pp. 296
ed. Adrian Ibbetseon, Beccy Watson and Maggie Ferguson

Contents

ACCESS AND INCLUSION IN LEISURE AND TOURISM

**LSA Publication No. 81. ISBN: 0 906337 92 5 [2003] pp. 288
eds. Bob Snape, Edwin Thwaites, Christine Williams**

Contents

VOLUNTEERS IN SPORT

LSA Publication No. 80. ISBN: 0 906337 91 7 [2003] pp. 107
ed. Geoff Nichols

Contents

LEISURE CULTURES: INVESTIGATIONS IN SPORT, MEDIA AND TECHNOLOGY

**LSA Publication No. 79. ISBN: 0 906337 90 9 [2003] pp. 221 + xii
eds. Scott Fleming and Ian Jones**

Contents

PARTNERSHIPS IN LEISURE:
SPORT, TOURISM AND MANAGEMENT

**LSA Publication No. 78. ISBN: 0 906337 89 5 [2002] pp. 245 + iv
eds. Graham Berridge and Graham McFee**

Contents

LEISURE STUDIES:
TRENDS IN THEORY AND RESEARCH

**LSA Publication No. 77. ISBN: 0 906337 88 7 [2001] pp. 198 + iv
eds. Stan Parker and Lesley Lawrence**

Contents

SPORT TOURISM: PRINCIPLES AND PRACTICE

LSA Publication No. 76. ISBN: 0 906337 87 9 [2001] pp. 174 + xii eds. Sean Gammin and Joseph Kurtzman

Contents

VOLUNTEERING IN LEISURE: MARGINAL OR INCLUSIVE?

LSA Publication No. 75. ISBN: 0 906337 86 0 [2001] pp. 158+xi
eds. Margaret Graham and Malcolm Foley

Contents

LEISURE CULTURES, CONSUMPTION AND COMMODIFICATION

**LSA Publication No. 74. ISBN: 0 906337 85 2 [2001] pp. 158+xi
ed. John Horne**

Contents

LEISURE AND SOCIAL INCLUSION: NEW CHALLENGES FOR POLICY AND PROVISION

**LSA Publication No. 73. ISBN: 0 906337 84 4 [2001] pp. 204
eds. Gayle McPherson and Malcolm Reid**

Contents

JUST LEISURE:
EQUITY, SOCIAL EXCLUSION AND IDENTITY

LSA Publication No 72. ISBN: 0 906337 83 6 [2000] pp. 195+xiv
Edited by Celia Brackenridge, David Howe and Fiona Jordan

Contents

JUST LEISURE:
POLICY, ETHICS & PROFESSIONALISM

LSA Publication No 71. ISBN: 0 906337 81 X [2000] pp. 257+xiv
Edited by Celia Brackenridge, David Howe and Fiona Jordan

Contents

WOMEN'S LEISURE EXPERIENCES: AGES, STAGES AND ROLES

LSA Publication No. 70. ISBN 0 906337 80 1 [2001]
Edited by Sharon Clough and Judy White

Contents

MASCULINITIES: LEISURE CULTURES, IDENTITIES AND CONSUMPTION

LSA Publication No. 69. ISBN: 0 906337 77 1 [2000] pp. 163

Edited by John Horne and Scott Fleming

Contents

GENDER ISSUES IN WORK AND LEISURE

LSA Publication No. 68.ISBN 0 906337 78 X
Edited by Jenny Anderson and Lesley Lawrence [pp. 173]

Contents

SPORT, LEISURE IDENTITIES AND GENDERED SPACES

LSA Publication No. 67. ISBN: 0 906337 79 8 [1999] pp. 196
Edited by Sheila Scraton and Becky Watson

Contents

HER OUTDOORS: RISK, CHALLENGE AND ADVENTURE IN GENDERED OPEN SPACES

LSA Publication No. 66 [1999] ISBN: 0 906337 76 3; pp. 131
Edited by Barbara Humberstone

Contents

POLICY AND PUBLICS

LSA Publication No. 65. ISBN: 0 906337 75 5 [1999] pp. 167
Edited by Peter Bramham and Wilf Murphy

Contents

CONSUMPTION AND PARTICIPATION: LEISURE, CULTURE AND COMMERCE

LSA Publication No. 64. ISBN: 0 906337 74 7 [2000]
Edited by Garry Whannel

Contents

GENDER, SPACE AND IDENTITY: LEISURE, CULTURE AND COMMERCE

LSA Publication No. 63. ISBN: 0 906337 73 9 [1998] pp. 191
Edited by Cara Aitchison and Fiona Jordan

Contents

THE PRODUCTION AND CONSUMPTION OF SPORT CULTURES: LEISURE, CULTURE AND COMMERCE

LSA Publication No. 62. ISBN: 0 906337 72 0 [1998] pp. 178
Edited by Udo Merkel, Gill Lines, Ian McDonald

Contents

TOURISM AND VISITOR ATTRACTIONS: LEISURE, CULTURE AND COMMERCE

LSA Publication No 61. ISBN: 0 906337 71 2 [1998] pp. 211
Edited by Neil Ravenscroft, Deborah Philips and Marion Bennett

Contents

LEISURE PLANNING IN TRANSITORY SOCIETIES

LSA Publication No. 58. ISBN: 0 906337 70 4
Edited by Mike Collins; pp 218

Contents

LEISURE, TIME AND SPACE: MEANINGS AND VALUES IN PEOPLE'S LIVES

LSA Publication No. 57. ISBN: 0 906337 68 2 [1998] pp. 198 + IV
Edited by Sheila Scraton

Contents

LEISURE, TOURISM AND ENVIRONMENT (I) SUSTAINABILITY AND ENVIRONMENTAL POLICIES

LSA Publication No. 50 Part I; ISBN 0 906337 64 X
Edited by Malcolm Foley, David McGillivray and Gayle McPherson (1999);

Contents

LEISURE, TOURISM AND ENVIRONMENT (II) PARTICIPATION, PERCEPTIONS AND PREFERENCES

LSA Publication No. 50 (Part II) ISBN: 0 906337 69 0; pp. 177+xii
Edited by Malcolm Foley, Matt Frew and Gayle McPherson

Contents

Editors' Introduction

LEISURE: MODERNITY, POSTMODERNITY AND LIFESTYLES

LSA Publications No. 48 (LEISURE IN DIFFERENT WORLDS Volume I)
Edited by Ian Henry (1994); ISBN: 0 906337 52 6, pp. 375+

Contents